Building Interpersonal Relationships through
TALKING, LISTENING, COMMUNICATING

Jeffrey S. Bormaster and Carol Lou Treat

8700 Shoal Creek Boulevard
Austin, Texas 78758

Library of Congress Cataloging in Publication Data

Bormaster, Jeffrey S., 1947–
    Building interpersonal relationships through talking,
listening, communicating.

    1. Interpersonal relations.   2. Interpersonal communi-
cation.   3. Group relations training.   4. Teacher-student
relationships.   I. Treat, Carol Lou, 1931–
II. Title.
HM132.B67   302.3   82–3702
ISBN 0-936104-26-0   AACR2

8700 Shoal Creek Boulevard
Austin, Texas 78758

10 9 8 7 6 5   89 90 91

Table of Contents

Preface

"Our leadership should be known not for the number of persons we dominate but for the number of personalities we enhance."

—a camp director for whom Carol Lou worked
many years ago

More and more as our population "explodes," our schools become larger and our student bodies spread out over more extensive areas, depersonalization and dehumanization tend to occur. In many schools students are assigned "student numbers" when they enter first grade, these numbers being their primary means of identification all through their public school years. And they are assigned to courses which have numbers and to teachers who have their own teacher numbers! At the end of the school day they return home to mothers and daddies who are identified by social security numbers and Master Card numbers and Exxon numbers.

Most teachers become teachers because they like young people, they want to share themselves and their knowledge and they are themselves people who are excited about learning. Most students need and want to have meaningful relationships with the adults in their lives. Most students need and want to have an especially close relationship with at least one of those adults who is his or her teacher. And this is the rationale for TLC (Talking, Listening, Communicating) groups.

The primary focus of TLC groups is human relations. Not only do teachers use human relations

techniques with their students, they must assist their students in using human relations techniques with others. Students, some more than others, must learn to cope with strong feelings such as love, hate, anger, fear. They need to develop tolerance and to understand intolerance. They need to develop in caring and sharing. Many need assistance in learning to understand and accept themselves. Studies indicate that one's success or lack of it is directly related to one's sense of self-worth. Young people who perceive themselves as *acceptable* tend to be *accepting*. Young people who see themselves as *able* and *responsible* tend to demonstrate *ability* and *responsible behavior*. Of course, the reverse is also true. Young people who view themselves negatively tend to respond negatively to people and to situations. Teachers, therefore, must attempt to gauge each student's self-perceptions by the barometer of his or her behavior, counteracting negative feelings by reinforcing positive images.

Obviously some students may have problems which require the expertise of a counselor, and these students need to be referred.

The goals of TLC groups are to develop positive regard for individual differences; to build a sense of belonging; to foster horizontal, non-authoritative relationships; and to maximize the development of human potential.

To assist teachers in leading TLC groups, a consistently organized curriculum was needed, one which was time-limited (all activities require 30 minutes or less), including clear teacher directions and masters for hand-outs and provided a sequenced variety of both pencil-and-paper and interactive activities. Since we could not find such a curriculum, we decided to write one.

The ideas for this book come from hundreds of resources, workshops and people as well as our own over thirty years as practitioners of our profession.

Introduction

Chapter One is designed to prepare you to be an effective group leader. The better your preparation, the more successful and less chaotic your group experience will be.

Following Chapter One, there are three sections of instructional activities organized into eight chapters. The chapters are sequenced, as are the activities within each chapter. The initial activities in each chapter are "low risk" and those toward the end of each chapter are higher risk.

The first section, composed of chapters 2 through 5, focuses on developing students' self-understanding, their ability to relate to and work with others and, ultimately, their functioning as members of a group. Each chapter in section one includes a series of:

A. *Short Warm Ups:* Dichotomies
Stems
These take fives minutes maximum and serve to bring the group together and set the stage for the activity.

B. *Discussions*
Included in each chapter are several topics we suggest for group discussion.

C. *Activities*
The series of activities are sequenced from simpler, low-risk to more complex, requiring more foundation. Based on your group of students you should determine which activities are appropriate. We have included both pencil-and-paper and non-pencil-and-paper activities.

D. *Dear TLC Group*
These letters serve as a way of concluding each chapter.

E. *Music and Poetry Expression*
Today's students are very much involved with music and poetry. To personalize learning, we suggest providing time for personal sharing.

The second section, composed of chapters 6 through 8, focuses on the development of creativity, problem solving and decision making skills through group processes. This section is based on the assumption that you already have a functioning group and you want to teach them the skills that will help them become action-oriented groups. The following are the decision making and problem solving models used in this curriculum guide.

Decision Making Model

Decision making can occur four different ways. Using majority rule, those who are in the majority win and those in the minority tend to feel that they lost.

Under minority rule, a select few "railroad" their desires through the group, leaving the majority feelings as though they had lost.

With authority rule, participants defer to an authority, possibly a teacher or some other person perceived as an authority. In this case many may not agree and thus they feel they lost in the decision making process.

Consensus is the decision making model we used. In consensus all participants buy into the decision. While this may take longer, working for a decision everyone accepts puts all into a win situation, thus assuring more support for the final decision.

Problem Solving Model

In the chapter on problem solving the activities are based on the problem solving process which:
1. Identifies what the problem is,
2. Generates possible solutions to the problem,
3. Selects the best solution,
4. Develops a plan to carry out the solution.

The final section, chapter 9, deals with how to end a TLC group. It is important that a group which has become a cohesive, sharing entity needs to come to a full sense of closure ... i.e., "we spent time together, shared and learned, and now it is over." The activities outlined in this chapter will help bring that all-important sense of closure to your group members.

BEFORE YOU BEGIN

You could begin immediately with the activities included in this curriculum guide. However, we feel a word of caution is needed. If you are prepared to lead TLC groups, you will find the results positive, exciting and rewarding for those in your group. Moving into the activities without being thoroughly prepared could cause significant harm.

Prepare yourself.

Protect your students.

The first chapter is designed to help you become a successful group leader. Read it. In it you will find a discussion on group structures, effective group leadership skills and hints on dealing with a variety of problems which could arise in leading a TLC group.

For your group to receive maximum benefit from the activity and from each other, each session should be processed. Chapter one ends with a discussion on processing and feedback, as well as sample feedback forms. The purpose of processing is to insure learnings are realized, thus eliminating a "fun and games" feeling. Feedback is to help you do a better job as group leader.

Take a little time and help insure a quality experience for your TLC group and for yourself.

1

Teacher: Preparing Yourself

The role of the teacher, or group leader, is critical to the success of the group. The model set by the teacher will set the model for participants/students to follow. To the extent possible, you should yourself participate in the activities. Remember, some activities allow this more than others do.

Your modeling needs to be nonjudgmental, open and caring. Avoid passing judgment on statements with which you may disagree. Help students avoid this, too.

In the affective area, there is no black and white, no final answer. Affective education allows exploration, examination, and discovery, unbounded by fact. Your role will be to facilitate and nurture that self-discovery process.

Often teachers say students only laugh and cut up. You set the tone for sessions, and if you are on too high-risk grounds, laughter and cutting-up are good indicators. If you treat the session like game time and do not value the time, so will students. Processing what they have learned will help students see value in the activities. Also, the value students find in a session will be the value modeled by you.

GROUP STRUCTURES

As will be noticed in this curriculum guide, various group structures are recommended for exercises. There are reasons for this. Some activities are better suited for large groups, some for small. Below are the structures and some advantages and disadvantages of each.

1. Dyads, Triads (pairs and threesomes)

Some of the exercises are designed for one person while the other observes, reacts or responds. Then their roles are reversed. A one-to-one relationship is usually much less threatening than speaking or acting out in a larger group. Also, there is obviously much more interpersonal involvement in a dyad. In triads, one person at a time usually acts as an observer while the other two engage in the exercise. An obvious disadvantage to dyads and triads is that the participants become involved with very few people, with minimal direct teacher monitoring.

2. Small Groups

Many of the activities in this guide are designed for groups of five or so. The reason for this is that a small group will enable each person to participate and receive responses from others. A disadvantage is that the leader/teacher has little direct control over a small group. Since many of the activities are for groups of five, the leader/teacher should attempt to vary the groupings from meeting to meeting unless specified otherwise.

3. Fishbowl (Inner and Outer Circles)

This structure is especially effective in teaching listening and responding skills. The inner circle (half of the group) is given a sentence stem or discussion topic to talk about. The other half, in an outer circle, listens without commenting, watching the group process in the inner circle. After a short time, they switch positions and the new group in the inner circle gets the opportunity to show how well they listened by responding to what they heard the others say. Then they are given a sentence stem or discussion topic, either the same one or a new one. The leader/teacher with inner and outer circles control over the group and the opportunity to model appropriate behavior when he or she is in the inner circle.

4. Large Group (25 or so)

This is a non-threatening group structure in which participants can feel free to participate or not. It affords them the opportunity to hear from many different people and respond to them. It also offers the leader considerable control and the chance to model appropriate behavior.

TEACHER/LEADER AND GROUP

The teacher/leader can further the goals of the group by remembering the following:

1. T.L.C. group meetings consist of three parts:
   a. Warm up
   b. Activity or exercise
   c. Processing (asking open-ended questions about content, learnings, feelings which enable students to realize what they have learned).

2. Help students make "I" statements, speaking for themselves and allowing others that right.

3. Remind students to speak directly *to* each other rather than *about* each other ("John, you seem ..." instead of "He seems...").

4. Encourage students to talk in terms of feelings.

5. Remind students, if it seems necessary, not to discuss individuals who are not present.

6. Remember, everyone has the right to be silent.

7. Serve as a model by:
   a. "Talking straight"

b. Trying to avoid asking questions which can be answered "yes" or "no"
c. Trying to determine the feeling behind a question.

8. Remember to ask for a response.

9. Remember always to process!

SKILLS FOR GROUP LEADERS

1. Active Listening
   • Remember and model non-verbal ways of listening such as eye contact, nodding appropriately, smiling, gestures, posture, etc.
   • Ask open-ended questions—"Would you like to tell us more about that?"—rather than direct questions which may be answered "yes" or "no."
   • Ask specific questions "tentatively," only if you are sure they are non-threatening and seen by the group member as helpful.
   • Ask specific questions when you are trying to help the group member clarify what he or she means.
   • Model the "okayness" of quiet, of allowing time for people to think.
   • Watch for group members' non-verbal signals—i.e., leaning forward, seeking eye contact with you as though they want to say something. "Do you have something you'd like to say, Jack?"
   • Keep the focus on the group members, not on yourself.

2. Focus on Feelings
   • Go from experience to feeling: "When that happened how did you feel about it?"
   • Accept all feelings as real without labeling them "good" or "bad." "You really felt that deeply." "It sounds like you're really concerned about that."
   • Notice when others seem to be identifying with feelings being expressed by a participant and give them the opportunity to talk about it. "You seemed so involved in what Donna was saying it was as though you'd had those same feelings yourself."
   • Observe the groups' reactions to a member's sharing and verbalize them. "The group really seemed to be with you, John."
   • Respond to words or phrases which might indicate strong feelings the participant was having. "When you told us about watching the moon's reflection on the water it sounded like you were feeling some really special feelings, Kay." Sometimes simply repeating a feeling

word or phrase will elicit more sharing from the person.

3. Give Recognition

- Look at each person gently and calmly when you speak to him or her.
- Learn each person's name and use it. If you forget a name, admit it and ask.
- Thank each participant for his or her contributions but don't make evaluative comments such as "that was good, Jack" because if you forget to comment on a contribution the group member may infer "that was bad." Non-verbal ways of thanking contributors—i.e., nodding, smiling, eye contact—may also be used.
- Praise good listening skills in others. "Your response, Linda, to what Michael just said showed you really were listening to him."
- Give positive reinforcement to people who share feelings—"It seemed as though that was really hard for you to talk about, Lisa, and it was neat that you could do so"—but not so effusively that others feel pressured to do the same. Make it "okay" *not* to share, too!

4. Respond

- Model responding skills—repeating verbatim what has just been said, paraphrasing it, adding on to it with a similar experience of your own or asking an open-ended question about it.
- Encourage participants to respond to each other. Too often group members address all their remarks to the leader because the leader is the only one who responds to them. "Mike, would you like to respond to what Jerry just said?"
- Help participants by supplying words for them if their hesitancy as they speak seems based upon a temporary "loss for words" and not reticence in sharing. Don't take over what they are saying, though!
- Stay "with" the participant. Don't stop his or her momentum by interrupting with a lot of questions.

5. Summarize

- From time to time, when the flow of conversation slows down or when several have spoken, ask for a review. "Let's see where we are now . . ." Ask if someone in the group would summarize what was said.
- Be able yourself to summarize what each person has said. At first you will need to model this skill. Later group members will be able to do this. You may need to help them. "Fred, I thought *this* is what you were saying . . ."
- Give positive reinforcement to group members whose responses and summaries show they were listening attentively.
- Review can be used when a group member has digressed from the topic. Without pointing out the digression and making him or her feel "put down," the leader may say "Thank you, Lisa. Now, let's see what we've talked about up till now."
- Leader or participants should summarize at the end of the meeting what has been discussed. Always address people directly—i.e., "Steve, you told us . . ." rather than "he said." Encourage group members to do this also. "Linda, could you say that to Steve?"

6. Focus on Similarities and Differences

- Help group members see their similarities to each other but also help them value their differences.
- Summarizing and paraphrasing flow naturally into focusing on similarities and differences. "Let's see where we are now. Mike, you said you . . . and Jack, it sounded like you were saying almost the same thing. . . ."
- Encourage participants to identify similarities and differences. "Is there sort of a pattern here? Can someone tell us if what we just heard sounded like what someone else said a little while ago?"
- Don't overdo discussion of similarities and differences! Let it occur naturally and when it seems appropriate.

7. Involve Everyone

- Let a reticent group member know that you would welcome his or her contributions but that it is "okay" to remain silent.
- Deal with disrupters gently. "You seem really angry today" or "You really seem like you would rather be somewhere else today" or "Is there anything we can do to help you feel more involved with us?"
- Watch for non-verbal signals that reticent members are wanting to be invited to talk. "Janet, you looked like you really wanted to say something then."
- Encourage reticent group members to respond to others and give positive reinforcement when they do so. "Marsha, you really seemed 'tuned in' to Janet just then. Could you respond to what she said?" "You really were listening closely!"
- Touch participants who are "acting out" while keeping eye contact with the one who is speaking. This frequently will quiet the disruptive participant. It may be necessary to separate two group members who are distracting each other's attention. Do this kindly. "Jack and Bruce, I'm having a hard time hearing over

your conversation. How about one of you moving over here?''

THINK ON THESE THINGS, GROUP LEADER

1. How do I like to be led?

   _____

   _____

   _____

   _____

2. Qualities which I like in people in positions of leadership:

   _____

   _____

   _____

   _____

   _____

   _____

   _____

3. Would I follow me?

   _____

   _____

PROCESSING

In order to reinforce the learning individuals acquire in a session, we suggest you build in time to process the experiences the group has had. In processing, it is important to talk about oneself. The questions we suggest with activities are first person, "I" questions. Groups need to be tightly monitored by the leader during this time to keep the group on task—sharing what one learned about him or her self.

GROUP LEADER FEEDBACK

It is important that the students in your groups feel that they can give you honest feedback about the way they experience your behavior toward them. It is also useful for you to know how your actions are perceived by your students. The following activities can be used to elicit feedback from your students.

1.1   HOW DO YOU SEE YOUR LEADER?

Material: One copy of master 1.1 "How Do You See Your Leader?" for each student.

Time: 5 minutes.

To the Teacher: As you lead groups, it is important to get feedback from group members on how you are doing. This activity should be done at the conclusion of a T L C session.

Directions to Teacher:

1. Explain to students that as you lead them through T L C activities, you are trying to be a good group leader.
2. Hand out one copy of "How Do You See Your Leader?" to each student and tell them that one way to be a better group leader is to get feedback. Ask students to give you that feedback anonymously by completing the form.
3. It should take 5 minutes to complete the forms and have them collected.

Note: To show students that you read their forms you may want to give them some feedback at a later session about what you plan to do differently as a result of their input.

1.2   PAY DAY

Materials: One copy of master 1.2, a blank check for each student.

Time: 5 minutes.

To the Teacher: This is a quick way to get feedback at the end of a T L C session on how well you are doing as a group leader.

Directions to Teacher:

1. Explain to students that you want to do as good a job as possible as group leader. Some people get paid according to how good a job they do.
2. Hand out a blank pay check to each student and ask them to pay you an amount between $0.00 and $10.00 based on how well you have done as their group leader. Tell students they don't need to sign the pay checks.
3. After 5 minutes, collect the pay checks.

1.2   PAY DAY (VARIATION)

Materials: Copies of form 1.2, one set of pay checks for each student equal to the number of persons in their group.

Time: 15 minutes.

To the Teacher: This exercise should only be used with groups who have been working together for a while and are a trusting working group.

Directions to Teacher:

1. Explain to students that some people get paid according to how good a job they do. They have

been a working group for some time, and it is pay day. Each student had $10.00 to divide among their group members. Write a check to each member of your group, distributing the $10.00 based on how good a job you think each did as a group member. Allow 5 minutes for writing checks.
2. After 5 minutes, hand out pay checks.
3. After everyone gets his or her checks, process in a large group: "How did it feel when you added up your pay checks?" "What is something you could/might do different next time to get a bigger pay check?"

1.3 TELEGRAM

Materials: One copy of master 1.3, 3 blank telegrams for each student.

Time: 10 minutes.

To the Teacher: The telegrams provide a way for sending positive feedback. This should be used at the end of a T L C session where students have been working in groups.

Directions to Teacher:
1. Begin by explaining that telegrams are used to send important messages to other people. Each of you will receive 3 blank telegrams with which to send positive messages to others. Your first telegram is to be a positive message to the person to your right; the second to the person to your left; the third to anyone else to whom you want to send a message. You will have 5 minutes to write your telegrams, but do not send them.
2. When everyone is ready or 5 minutes are up ask everyone to deliver their telegrams and read the ones they receive.
3. Form a large group and process. "How did you feel when you read your telegrams?"

1.4 GOING HOME

Materials: None.

Time: 15–25 minutes.

To the Teacher: The purpose of this activity is to help students summarize what they did. This is an excellent end of the day/session activity.

Directions to Teacher:
1. Ask students to get in groups of six and to sit so they can hear each other.
   Note: If this activity follows a small group activity, use the group that is already formed.

2. Explain to students that this activity is to help them answer the question: "What did you do today?"
3. Ask students to close their eyes and as you talk, to imagine what they would say.
   "Today we have done some activities for us. Today is over and you are going home. You leave school and return to your home. Upon your arrival one of your parents greets you and asks, "What did you learn today at school?"
4. Ask students to open their eyes and share with their groups what they told their parent.
5. After 5 minutes, ask each group to develop a list of group learnings to be shared.
6. After 5 minutes, have each group report their learnings to the total group.
7. Process. "How do you feel about sharing your day with your folks?" "How do your parents usually feel about what you do at school?"

1.5 YOU WERE THERE

Materials: None.

Time. 10 minutes.

To the Teacher: This activity helps students refocus on what happened earlier, and will help them focus for today's activities.

Directions to Teacher.:
1. Ask students to form groups of five each.
2. Explain that on T.V. there used to be a show "You Were There." What the show did was take you back to earlier events in history as though you were there. Each group will have 5 minutes to create a 30-second "You Were There" spot on our last T L C session.
3. After 5 minutes, ask any groups who want to, to present their "You Were There at Our Last Meeting" to the entire group.
4. Process. "Were you pleased that you remembered the last meeting so well?" "How did someone who was absent last time feel about hearing 'You Were There?'"

1.6 TOAST TO SUCCESS

Materials: None.

Time: 10 minutes.

To the Teacher: This activity provides a way for giving positive feedback to a group. It should be done as a closure activity to a group session.

Directions to Teacher: (Students should already have been in groups of 4–6.)

1. Explain that on special occasions like weddings people offer a toast to the occasion. Toasts are a way of saying "Good job!"
2. Model a toast to the group.
   e.g., for listening so well
   or
   for working in groups.
3. Ask each member to give a toast to their group focusing on something special/positive the group has done.
4. After the toasts, in larger groups, process. "What made toasting difficult or easy for you?" "How did you feel as part of the group being toasted?" "What does this say about feedback and groups?"

1.7 PRAISE

Materials: One copy of master 1.7 "Praise List" for each student.

Time: 20 minutes.

To the Teacher: Words we generally use to give positive feedback have little meaning. "Good," "Fine," "Great," while being positive aren't specific. The intent of this activity is to teach students how to give meaningful praise.

Directions to Teacher:

1. Ask students to get in groups of four.
2. Explain that praise is often given but usually is not meaningful.
   e.g., a "Good" on a paper doesn't mean as much as: "This is a better paper than last time. All your sentences are in complete form. Good for you!"
3. Hand out the Praise List and ask each group to turn the praise words into more meaningful praise statements. Do as many as they can.
4. Stop after 15 minutes and have each group report one or two they changed.
5. In a large group process. "What did you learn about giving praise?"

STEMS TO CONNECT SESSIONS

These stems provide continuity between group meetings. They allow students to get reconnected. Use only one stem per session. You can use the same stem over.

Directions to Teacher: At the start of a session, ask students, in turn, to complete the sentence you'll begin.

Possible Stems:

1. What I remember from last session is _____.
2. My feeling about last time is _____.
3. My hope for today is _____.
4. My expectation for today is _____.
5. My high point last time was _____.
6. One thing I learned last session was _____.

2

Understanding Self

2.1 DICHOTOMIES

Materials: None.

Time: 5 minutes.

To the Teacher: The purpose of "Dichotomies" is to help students think about themselves and their values. As an initial activity in a session, "Dichotomies" serves as an icebreaker. Use only 3–4 dichotomies which are relevant to the day's session.

Directions to Teacher:

1. Create a large open area for students to move about.
2. Explain to students that you will give them a set of words. Each end of the space represents one of the words. When you say the set of words, ask them to move from room center to the end that represents the word with which they identify.
3. Give students an example.

Step 1
Students stand center

Step 2
Give choices
    Are you HOT ...   ... or COLD

Step 3
Students move

	Students	
HOT	move to	COLD
	either end	

Step 4
Ask students to notice what their choices were, who made the same choice and to share with one other person why they made this choice.

Possible Dichotomies for SELF

open	or	closed
wall		window
race car		VW
gold bonded		diamond studded
people		thing
happy		sad
lover		fighter
country western		rock & roll
peace		war
cigarette		drink
physical		mental
winner		loser
dull		interesting
island		bridge
cowboy		hippy
caring		cranky
positive		negative
day		night
spring		fall
active		passive
real		fake

laugher	cryer
yes	no
ping pong ball	paddle

2.2 STEMS

Materials: None.

Time: 10 minutes per stem.

To the Teacher: The purpose of "Stems" is to structure positive responses using sentence stems. Any student should be allowed to pass. Use only one stem per session. Choose one which is relevant to the day's session.

Directions to Teacher:

1. Ask students to form a circle with you.
2. Explain that you are going to start a sentence and you would like for each student in turn to complete it. If a student chooses to pass, make passing acceptable.
3. Give an example by saying the sentence stem, then repeat the sentence stem and complete it yourself. (Your completion will model for the students.)
4. In a structured way (left to right) ask each student to say the start of the sentence (important!) and to complete it.

> Examples:
> Teacher (stem) "I feel good when . . ."
> Teacher (completion) "I feel good when people say positive things to me."
> Student "I feel good when. . ." (Ask to make stem into full sentence.)
> Student "I feel good when I go home."

Stems

One thing I like about me _____.
One thing that makes me happy _____.
I am proud that I _____.
I feel good when _____.
I get excited when _____.
My clothes say I'm _____.
Something I do well _____.
My greatest strength is _____.
Someone I'd like to be like _____.
I feel comfortable when _____.
I'm good at _____.
I feel different from other people because _____.
How I react when I'm successful _____.
Seeing good results from my behavior _____.
Something which gives me a feeling of power _____.
When I feel I've done a good job I _____.
My favorite way to get praise is _____.
My way to get attention from others is _____.

The way I solved a problem I had was _____.
Something I'd like to change about myself _____.

2.3 SAYINGS

Materials: None.

Time: 20 minutes.

To the Teacher: The purpose of "SAYINGS" is to have students examine some famous and not-so-famous sayings, and discuss the meanings of those sayings and see if they have application to their lives.

Directions to Teacher:

1. Have students sit together in groups of five.
2. Give each group a saying from the list below. Have one student in each group read the statement to his/her group. Small groups discuss what the saying means and how it might apply to them as individuals. PRACTICE LISTENING AND RESPONDING SKILLS.
3. After fifteen minutes, get students back into a large group, seated in a circle.
4. Process. "Would any of the groups like to report what you decided the statement means?" "Did another group find some other meaning?" "Would someone like to share what this statement says to him or her?"

Sayings-Self

"Today is the first day of the rest of your life."
"A person wrapped up in himself makes a very small package."
"We see things not as they are but as we are."
"There is a great deal of unmapped country within us."
"I am a part of all I have met."
"When a man finds not repose in himself it is in vain for him to seek it elsewhere."
"Use the talents you possess, for the woods would be very silent if no birds sang except the best."
"A talent is formed in silence, but a character in the stream of the world."
"A piece of charcoal loses its blackness only when fire penetrates it."
"You may not always be better than others. You can always be better than yourself."
"Character is what you are in the dark."
"The man who does not read good books has no advantage over the man who can't read them."
"What you are to be you now are becoming."

2.4 BRAINSTORMING

Materials: Sheet of paper and pencil for each group.

Time: 15 minutes.

To the Teacher: The purpose of this activity is to encourage students to think of and list as many meanings of the word "SELF" as they can so they don't get locked into simply one definition.

Directions to Teacher:

1. Get students into groups of five and have them select a recorder. Give paper and pencil to recorder.
2. Remind students of the rules of brainstorming.
   a. Quantity, not quality, is important.
   b. No discussion or judgments.
   c. Free-wheel, add onto each other's ideas.
3. Tell recorders to write "SELF" at the top of their papers.
4. Tell students "You have three minutes to think of as many meanings as you can for 'SELF'."
5. Stop after three minutes. Ask each group to report on the number of ideas they came up with and to share a couple with everyone. (Praise creativity and productiveness.)
6. Bring students back into a large circle to process. "Did you feel good about your contribution to your group's list?" "Are there any new ways you think now about "SELF" that you'd like to share with us?"

2.5 "SELF" DISCUSSION

Materials: None.

Time: 20 minutes.

To the Teacher: For teachers and students who like a discussion format the topics related to this section will serve as a basis for structuring learning through discussion.

Directions to Teacher:

1. Have students sit in one large circle with you.
2. Explain that you would like to have a discussion. The discussion has no ending. There is no one right or wrong answer. Remind students of the rules for group discussion (especially that only one person talk at a time so that everyone can be heard).
3. Introduce the topic and facilitate group interaction.
4. At the end of the discussion, ask for someone to summarize the discussion.
5. Process. "One way this discussion was of value to me is _____."

Discussion Topics:

1. "A lot of people say it is important we know ourselves. What is self? Do we need to know ourselves?"
2. "Are your own feelings important?"
3. "How do we learn who we are?"

2.6 ANIMAL FANTASY

Materials: None.

Time: 30 minutes.

To the Teacher: The purpose of this activity is to get students to begin sharing in a nonthreatening way who they are and are not.

Directions to Teacher:

1. Ask students to sit in a large circle.
2. Ask students (and yourself) to write down the animal each would most like to be and the animal he or she would least like to be. Explain that you will ask everyone to share what their choices are and why they made those choices.
3. Beginning with yourself, share in a large group. (Your model will set the tone for the group.)
4. After everyone who wanted to has shared, ask students to complete the following stem: "One thing I learned about myself today in sharing is _____"
(Again teacher should begin in order to model.)

2.7 SELF: ADJECTIVES

Materials: Copy of master 2.7, Self Adjective List, for every student.

Time: 20 minutes.

To the Teacher: In this exercise, students describe themselves to others through selecting self descriptors.

Directions to Teacher:

1. Explain to students that often it is hard for us to think of the words we would use to best describe ourselves. Each student will get an adjective list and select the six that best describe him or herself.
2. Hand out lists and give students ten minutes to choose only six adjectives.
3. Call time after ten minutes. Have students get into a circle of 6–10 and share their six words. (As an option, if you have time, do the sharing in one circle.)
4. After everyone has shared, ask students to discuss in one large circle if the exercise helped them get to know other students.

Note: You may repeat this exercise asking students to choose the six they would most like to be described as.

2.8 MY COAT OF ARMS

Materials: One copy of master 2.8, My Coat of Arms, for each student, crayons or colored pens.

Time: 15 minutes.

To the Teacher: This activity helps students think about who they are, what they are doing with their lives, whether or not what they are doing is making a difference. Emphasize that art ability doesn't matter; what counts is that the student knows what he or she is trying to express.

Directions to Teacher:

1. Give each student a blank shield. Have students sit in groups of five perhaps around a table with the materials on the table.
2. Write questions on the board as follows:
   1. What is your greatest achievement up until now?
   2. What is your family's greatest achievement?
   3. What is one thing other people can do to make you happy?
   4. What do you want to become?
   5. Draw three things you are good at.
   6. What is a personal motto you live by?
3. Instruct students that they are to draw on the appropriate area on their coat of arms, a picture, design, or symbol which represents their answers on the above questions. Only number six can be expressed in words!
4. When they have finished, let them share—IF THEY WISH—their coats of arms with each other.
5. Then collect coats of arms and post them around the room or on bulletin boards at a later time.
6. In a large circle, process. "Did you learn anything new about yourself?"

2.9 "I AM" COLLAGE

Materials: Many old magazines, one large piece of paper per student, paste.

Time: 30 minutes to make, 10 minutes to share.

To the Teacher: The purpose of this activity is to help students think about who they are, what they're like, how they feel about themselves, and to share this with the group.

Directions to the Teacher:

1. Place materials in a central location, easily accessible to all.
2. Give each student a large piece of paper and ask that they write "I AM" in the center of their paper.
3. Have students go through magazines, find pictures or words which describe them, tear them out and paste them on "I AM" paper. Allow 30 minutes to do.
4. At second session, have them sit in a large circle and share their "I AM" collages with the group. They may explain them or not, whichever they prefer.
5. In a large group, process. "How did you feel, trying to find the pictures?" "Was it easy?" "Why?" "Why not?" "How was it to share yourself in this way?"

2.10 A DESCRIPTION OF ME

Materials: Multicolors of construction paper.

Time: 30 minutes.

To the Teacher: In this activity, each participant is to choose several sheets of construction paper and make something that describes what he or she is.

Directions to Teacher:

1. Explain to students that they will be making something that describes what they are. They should consider both the color of paper they choose and what they make out of it. They may not use anything else.
2. Have students select several sheets of paper and get busy.
3. After fifteen minutes, have students get into groups of six and share their creations as expressions of what they are like.
4. Process. "How was it to try to decide how to express yourself this way?"

2.11 "ME" PICTURE

Materials: Large piece of paper and crayon or magic marker for each participant.

Time: 20–30 minutes.

To the Teacher: The purpose of the "ME" Picture is to focus on the person we are and to try to symbolize, in some way, our SELF and to be able to explain it to others.

Directions to the Teacher:

1. Give each student a piece of paper and crayon or magic marker.
2. Ask each student to close his or her eyes and think silently about the person he or she is, what they're like, what they stand for, etc. Try to think of some symbol which best represents them, a symbol other than a word.

3. Instruct them to open their eyes and draw that symbol on their paper.
4. Get into a large circle and, in turn around the circle, let each hold his symbol up and explain it.
5. After each has had a turn, process. "Was it easy to think of a symbol or did many things go through your mind?" "How did it feel when it was getting close to your turn to hold your symbol up and explain it?" "Did you like sharing your SELF this way?"

2.12 GETTING TO KNOW ME

Materials: None.

Time: 20 minutes.

To the Teacher: The purpose of this activity is to encourage students to notice things they have in common with other members of the group and one thing which makes them unique.

Directions to Teacher:

1. Have students sit in a large circle.
2. Ask them to look around and notice ways in which they are alike and different from the rest of the group.
3. Explain that you'd like for everyone to think of one positive thing that makes them unique or different.
4. Give an example yourself (make it positive about yourself):
   - You are a teacher, everyone else is a student, or
   - You are the oldest, or
   - You are the tallest, or, etc.
4. After everyone has shared, ask students if they remember what people said.
6. Have students say, in a large group, what they heard others say.
7. Afterwards, ask students how they felt when they told their uniqueness and when they heard someone else tell it back.

2.13 GROWING

Materials: None.

Time: 10–15 minutes.

To the Teacher: This activity will help students get in touch with who they actually are, what their goals are as individuals, what they are doing now to become the sort of people they want to be.

Directions to Teacher:

1. Get students into groups of five.
2. Tell students: "I'm going to ask you a couple of

questions which I want you to close your eyes and think about. After a few minutes I'd like for you to share your answers with the other members of your small group. Be sure to really listen to each other, and practice responding to each other so they'll know you've really listened. The questions I want each of you to answer, first to yourself, then to your small group, are: 'In what ways am I a better person this week than I was last week?' 'In what ways am I *growing*?' (Repeat questions again.) Okay, think about yourself now, and when you know your answers, wait until the other members of your group seem ready to share their answers before you begin your discussion."
3. Have students get back into a large circle. Process. "Did you identify some real changes going on in you, to become the sort of person you want to be?" "Who'd like to share your answers with us?" (Thank sharers.) "How does it feel to see yourself as growing toward some goals?"

2.14 MILLIONAIRE

Materials: None.

Time: 10–15 minutes.

To the Teacher: This activity will help students think about themselves and their values.

Directions to Teacher:

1. Get students into a large circle.
2. Say: "Do you all remember the TV show, 'The Millionaire?' We're going to pretend today that I've suddenly become both very wealthy and very generous and I've decided to give each of you one thousand dollars. Think about it! One thousand dollars! The only stipulation is that you *must* spend the entire sum—$1000—on *yourself*. Now, who'd like to tell us what you'd do with your thousand dollars? Would someone else like to share with us how you'd spend *your* money? Let's remember to listen to each other, and to respond to each other." (Spend seven or eight minutes in discussion.)
3. Process. "Did you learn something new about yourself now that you're 'rich'?" "Would someone like to share what you discovered?" "How'd it feel to be told you *had* to spend it on yourself? Why?"

2.15 CAUSES

Materials: None.

Time: 15–20 minutes.

To the Teacher: This activity will help students think about their values, what causes them to believe in them so strongly that they'd be willing to die for them. When they discuss a cause they'd be willing to live for, it *should* be the same.

Directions to Teacher:

1. All students should be grouped in one large circle.
2. Say to students: "A lot of the activities we've engaged in, in our small and large groups, have caused us to look at our values, what is important to us. Today I want us to think about a *cause* that we'd be willing to die for. Who would like to begin the discussion? And let's all try to remember to really listen to each other and to respond to each other in a way that lets the person know we really heard him or her."
3. After six or seven minutes, say: "Okay, now let's talk about a cause we'd be willing to *live* for . . . a cause we'd be willing to *live* for. Who'd like to begin?"
4. After five minutes, process. "Anybody like to share something you just discovered about yourself?" "Is it easier to say we'd be willing to die for something than to live for it?" "Why is that, do you think?"

2.16   TWENTY THINGS

Materials: Copy of master 2.16, Twenty Things, for each student.

Time: 15 minutes.

To the Teacher: This is a personal inventory which is especially valuable when repeated at infrequent intervals through the year (three or four times). If students will date and save their sheets, further valuable insights can be gained by comparing the three or four sheets at the end of the year. This inventory helps students think about things they really like to do and to see how and where they set their priorities.

Directions to Teacher:

1. Hand out the "Twenty Things" sheets and ask students to fill in quickly as many things as they can think of that they love to do. (Try to get twenty. More is okay.) Tell them this is private writing, that no one will be forced to share his or her list with anyone.
2. When students have finished their lists, ask that they search for patterns by coding their lists in the following way: In the first column, write *A* if you prefer to do the activity alone, *O* if you prefer to do it with others. In the second column, write $ for each activity that costs more than

five dollars a time. In the third column, write a minus sign (-) for any activity that you expect to be missing from your list five years from now. In the fourth column, write *P* for each activity that you think would occur in one of your parent's lists. In the fifth column check each activity that you have done within the past week. Finally, circle any activity which you have not done within the last year.
3. Tell students to keep the lists, that they'll get to do it again, and it will be interesting to compare them with each other.
4. Process. "Was there something I learned about myself?" "Did I learn anything about what I love to do?"

Note: Repeat this exercise later on and process how students have changed.

2.17   MY IDEAL DAY

Materials: None.

Time: 15–20 minutes.

To the Teacher: This will enable students to think about themselves, who they are, what they like to do, and whom, if anyone, they want with them.

Directions to Teacher:

1. Have everyone form one large circle. Tell them: "We are going to get into a fantasy, using our imaginations. What I want you to do is to close your eyes and really listen to what I say, really get into your own feelings and let yourself *go* completely with the 'task.' Close your eyes now, and think about an ideal day for you, something really perfect in every way. You've just awakened in the morning . . . the night's sleep has left you feeling absolutely great . . . you're in tip-top health . . . the weather is perfect . . . you have a whole day before you . . . a day in which to do anything you want to do . . . by yourself or with others . . . an IDEAL DAY . . . all yours . . . enough money, if you need money . . . enough time . . . think about it . . . feel the feelings you'd have with an IDEAL DAY before you . . . remember, nothing is impossible on this *ideal day* . . . (be silent for about five minutes) . . . now, in another couple of minutes I'm going to ask you to open your eyes very slowly and remain very quiet . . . stay with your IDEAL DAY (wait quietly two more minutes). Now open your eyes . . . remain silent . . . (use very quiet tone of voice). Would someone like to share with us your ideal day?" (Thank the sharers.) "Did anyone discover something you didn't know before about yourself, something you'd be willing to

share with us?" "Did anyone find he or she really would spend the day pretty much the same as any other day?" "Whose IDEAL DAY was really different, really far out?"

2.18 YESTERDAY

Materials: None.

Time: 20 minutes.

To the Teacher: The purpose of this activity is to have students reflect on one single event from their lives and its effect on them.

Directions to Teacher:

1. Have students get into groups of four.
2. Ask the following: "If you could choose one yesterday to live over, either again as it was or to change, what day would it be?" "How would you change it?"
3. Ask students to describe the day to their group, taking only two minutes each to describe their day. At the end of each two-minute period, have the group members repeat back to the speaker what he or she said.
4. Do four rounds so everyone speaks, repeating two-minute–one-minute cycle.
5. In a large group, process. "How did you feel about sharing?" "How did you feel when you heard what you said?"

2.19 PIE OF LIFE

Materials: Paper and pencil for each person.

Time: 15 minutes.

To the Teacher: This activity gets us to inventory our lives, to see how and where we invest our time. Stress to students that there are no "right" or "wrong" ways to divide a pie, that each of us lives a different life.

Directions to Teacher:

1. Students are seated in groups of five where they can see the board. The teacher draws a large circle on the board and says: "This circle represents a day in your life. You will divide it into four quarters by making dotted lines with each quarter containing six hours. Now think about how many hours you spend on a regular school day in each of the following areas:
   a. sleep
   b. school
   c. work, at a job that earns you money
   d. with friends, playing or talking
   e. on homework
   f. alone, playing, watching TV, reading, prac-

ticing a musical instrument
   g. on chores around the house
   h. with family, including meals
   i. on other pasttimes
2. Tell students to estimate how they spend all 24 hours. Draw an example on the board.

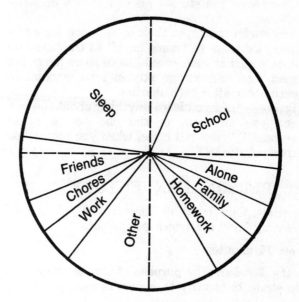

3. Ask students to draw their *own* "pies" and share them with their groups.
4. Process. "Are you satisfied with where you've invested your time?" "Is there anything you want to begin to do differently to change the size of some of your slices?"

2.20 PERSONAL LIFE MAP

Materials: None.

Time: 15 minutes.

To the Teacher: This will help students think about who and what they are now, their goals, and the sort of people they want to become.

Directions to Teacher:

1. Have the entire group seated in a large circle.
2. Ask students to close their eyes. Then say: "In your mind's eye, draw an imaginary road map on the inside of your eyelids. On the left side of the map is where you are now, not so much in terms of location but where you are in your life—your feelings, your awareness of yourself. On the right side of the map is where you want to go. Get in touch with both these areas. Think about the sort of person you want to become, the feelings you want to some day have about yourself. In the middle of your map, you may notice some

obstacles that block you from getting where you want to go. See if there is anything you can do about them now. If not, don't try to change them. Just be aware of what they are and how you feel about them now."
3. Be silent for five minutes or so. Teacher also closes eyes and studies his or her own personal life map.
4. Ask students to open their eyes. Pause for a moment for them to "come back" to the here and now. Ask if anyone would like to share his or her road map. Encourage students to respond to each other after each sharing.
5. Process. "Did you learn anything about the person you are now, or the one you want to become?" "How did it feel when you focused on those obstacles?"

2.21 PERSONAL INVENTORY

Materials: One copy of master 2.21 "Personal Inventory" and one pencil per person.

Time: 15 minutes.

To the Teacher: The purpose of this activity is to help students identify their own resources.

Directions to Teacher:

1. Students should be in groups of five. Give each a "Personal Inventory" sheet.
2. Have students fill out sheets with the information requested.
3. Ask students to share with others what they wrote and to compare the resources they have with those of their classmates.
4. If there is time, small groups might like to talk about three years ago, what resources they had then, and five years from now, what skills, knowledge, attitudes they hope to develop. How could they develop those resources?

2.22 AM I SOMEONE WHO?

Materials: Copy of master 2.22, "Am I Someone Who?", and pencil for each student.

Time: 15 minutes.

To the Teacher: This activity will help students concentrate on their values, on what they want out of their lives, and on what kind of people they want to become.

Directions to Teacher:

1. Students are in a large circle, each with a pencil and something (book or notebook, perhaps) in their laps to write upon *or* they may make a circle with their desks.

2. Tell students you are going to hand out a questionnaire and emphasize that there are no "right" or "wrong" answers. Encourage students to try to answer all questions as they *might* apply to them, using very few "maybe's."
3. Have students work silently on circling Y for "yes," N for "no," and M for "Maybe" on their papers.
4. When all seem to be finished, ask who would like to share the first one with the group. When one has done so, let another respond to him before going on to the next question.

> *Example:*
> Teacher: "Would someone like to read number one to us and how he or she answered it?"
> Student A: "Am I Someone who needs to be alone? Yes."
> Student B: "_____, I heard you say you need to be alone."
> Teacher: "Thank you, A, for sharing that with us, and B for letting A know you listened to him/her. Now, who would like to read question two and his/her answer?

5. After all questions have been read aloud and their answers shared with the group, process. "Did you find out something you had not known about yourself? "How did it make you feel when others listened carefully to your answer?"

2.23 PERSON OF THE YEAR

Materials: Paper, pencil for each participant.

Time: 15 minutes.

To the Teacher: This experience will help students think about themselves, what they are proud of, and what they like about themselves.

Directions to Teacher:

1. Students are in groups of five.
2. Tell students: "Each year some of our most popular magazines put on their cover the picture of the Person of the Year. Also, they have a feature article inside the magazine which tells all about that person—why he or she was selected as the outstanding person for that entire year. Each of us will decide, if we were to be chosen Person of the Year, what magazine would select us? Would it be PEOPLE? or EBONY? or SPORTS ILLUSTRATED? Let's pretend it is one of those three. Fold your piece of paper in half and draw the name of the magazine and your picture on the 'cover.' Don't worry about art work. Then on the inside, write what a magazine would say about you if you were their 'Per-

son of the Year.' Think about your strengths, about what you are proud of. If you wish, you may pretend you are older than you are now, that you actually have become the person you want to be! Write about that person.!"

3. After students have finished, let them share their "magazine" in their groups.

4. Process. "How did it feel to pretend you had been chosen for this honor?" "How did it feel to write about yourself, and to share it with the others in your group?"

2.24 MIRROR

Materials: None.

Time: 10 minutes.

To the Teacher: The purpose of "Mirror' is to reflect the good or positive strengths a person sees in him or herself.

Directions to Teacher:

1. Have each student pick another student with whom to pair off.

2. Have these dyads spread themselves out in an open space.

3. In dyads:
   a. Person A tells four things he really likes about him or herself.
   b. Person B responds to A: "What I heard you say you like about yourself are . . ."
   c. Person B tells four things he or she really likes about him or herself.
   d. Person A responds to B as in b.

4. Have students get back into a large circle to process. "How did it feel to say positive things about yourself?" "What did you learn about yourself in this exercise?"

2.25 "PROUD" EXERCISE

Materials: None.

Time: 15 minutes.

To the Teacher: This activity helps students become aware of the degree to which they are proud of their beliefs and actions and will make them want to do more things in which they can take pride.

Directions to Teacher:

1. Students and teacher are seated in a circle. Teacher will ask students to think of what they are proud of about themselves.

2. Teacher will ask questions (see following list) and students will respond in complete sentences (i.e., "I'm proud of . . ." or "I'm proud that . . ."

3. Any student may pass if he wishes. Teacher, be

very supportive of those who pass.

4. Teacher should emphasize that expressing pride is not boasting or bragging, that it simply means something we feel good about in ourselves.

5. Process. "How did it feel to tell the group you felt proud of something?" "Did this exercise cause you to learn anything about yourself?"

"Proud" Exercise

Sample Questions:

1. What is something you are proud of that you can do on your own?
2. What is something you are proud of in relation to money?
3. What are you proud of here at school?
4. What are you proud of about your gift giving?
5. What are you proud of in relation to your family?
6. What is something you have done about the ecology issue that you are proud of?
7. What is something you have written or drawn of which you are proud?
8. Is there any new skill you have learned in the past month or year?
9. Is there a decision you made about which you are proud?
10. Is there anything you have done for an older person?
11. Is there something you have made with your own hands?
12. Is there a musical instrument you play well?
13. Is there a habit you have worked hard to overcome, and succeeded?
14. Is there a dangerous thing you tried and succeeded at?
15. Is there something you did to help a new kid at school or in your neighborhood?
16. Is there anything you did to contribute to racial understanding?
17. Was there a time when you were an important example for a younger child?
18. Is there something you did to help a teacher?
19. Is there something in athletics about which you are especially proud?
20. Is there anything you have done to add to the beauty in this world?
21. Was there a time when you influenced others *not* to do something they were about to do?
22. Is there a funny thing you said or did?

(Think of some more of your own.)

2.26 COMMERCIAL

Materials: None.

Time: 25 minutes.

To the Teacher: This activity will help students to think about positive aspects of themselves—their ideas, attitudes, skills, etc.—and to share them or "sell" them to others.

Directions to Teacher:

1. Have students get into groups of five.
2. Say to students: "Each of us has some things we really like about ourselves. These may be ideas or attitudes, values we hold, skills we have, anything you can think of about yourselves that you really like. We have also heard commercials on the radio, some singing, some talking. Close your eyes for a few minutes and think about your self, what you really like about this person you call 'me,' and then create a talking or singing commercial which you can deliver to your group. You have ten minutes to do this."
3. After ten minutes (or earlier if groups seem to be ready to share), as groups to begin sharing their commercials, one at a time.
4. Get students back into a large circle to process. "Was it fun to think only of positive things about yourself?" "Who had a really good talking commercial they would like to share with the group?" "How about a singing one?"

2.27   EPITAPH

Materials: Pencil and paper for each student.

Time: 15 minutes.

To the Teacher: The purpose of this activity is to help students focus on what sorts of people they are and how they feel about themselves.

Directions to Teacher:

1. Ask students, arranged in groups of five, to draw a large tombstone on their papers.
2. Then, following the example of the inscriptions on old tombstones, complete this line in fifteen words or less:
      "Here lies . . ."
3. Have students share their epitaphs on a voluntary basis.
4. Process. "Did you discover anything about yourself you would like to share?"

2.28   AD FOR MY SELF

Materials: 1 large piece of paper per person, stacks of magazines, paste.

Time: 15 minutes.

To the Teacher: The purpose of this activity is to get students to concentrate on their strengths, to think about the things they like about themselves, and to try to "sell" their selves to others.

Directions to Teacher.

1. Have students work in groups of five with magazines, paste and paper easily accessible to each group.
2. Ask students to think about advertisements they see in newspapers, on TV and in magazines. Then, pick out words and pictures from magazines which will sell others on their outstanding characteristics, positive qualities, or value to others and paste them on their paper to make "an advertisement for my self."
3. Have students share their advertisements with others in their group.
4. Process. "How did you feel, looking through magazines for things which you value in your self?"

2.29   ONE QUESTION

Materials: None.

Time: 30 minutes.

To the Teacher: This activity helps students focus on an area they would be interested in learning more about. Not only does this activity give insight into the person, but is also a source of personal motivation.

Directions to Teacher:

1. Have students seated in groups of six.
2. Give them the following "suppose": "Suppose you could ask one question and be guaranteed a completely honest total answer and no one would know you asked it. What question would you ask and of whom? Share your question with your small group."
3. After sharing, bring students into a large circle and process. "What kinds of questions do we value most?" "How do you feel when you do not get an honest answer?"

(An alternative would be to make the question more specific: a question you might ask yourself, your friends, teachers, adults, parents, friends, etc.)

2.30   ALTER EGO

Materials: Copy of master 2.30, Alter Ego Profile Sheets, pencils for each student.

Time: 15 minutes.

To the Teacher: This will get students in touch with their ideal selves and will cause interaction and sharing with others.

Directions to Teacher:

1. Give each student a profile sheet. Say: "If you were your alter ego, your free spirit, your other

self, where would you live, what would be your choice of occupations, your hobbies, your daily bread, your choices in magazines, books, records, entertainment? What kind of clothes would you wear and what kind of house would you live in? What kind of car would you own? Remember, your alter ego is free from all your real responsibilities, duties, and relationships. You may wish to add the names of several famous people, living, dead, or fictional, that would make up a list of closest friends for your alter ego."

2. After sheets are filled out, divide the class into groups of seven and choose one student in each group to be the leader. The leader collects the Alter Ego Profile sheets, including his or her own, from the members of the group. He shuffles them and then reads each one anonymously. After each reading, members of the group try to guess the author of that Alter Ego Profile sheet.
3. Process. "What did you learn about yourself as you thought about having an alter ego?" "How did you feel when your fellow group members guessed your profile sheet correctly?" "How did it feel if no one guessed yours?"

2.31   I HAVE A DREAM

Materials: None.

Time: 10–30 minutes.

To the Teacher: This is a fantasy self disclosure activity which makes it okay for students to have wishes and provides a safe way to share them.

Directions to Teacher:

1. You can either do this as a total group in one circle or in small groups of 6–8 students.
2. Ask students if they ever heard of a man named Martin Luther King and what he is famous for. (Discuss 2–5 minutes.)
3. Say, "King is famous because he had a dream. We all have dreams. What is yours?"
4. Have students share their dreams.
5. After everyone has shared, process in a large group. "What did you learn in the activity?" "How did you feel saying your dream?" "How did you feel hearing others' dreams?"

2.32   RESUMÉ

Materials: Paper, pencil for each student. Copies of a real resumé, if available.

Time: 30 minutes.

To the Teacher: The purpose of this activity is to enable students to examine their strengths, think about how they might be used in a job and share them with others.

Directions to Teacher:

1. Have students work in small groups of 5–8. Explain to them the function of a resumé in jobseeking and show them a real one, if available. Brainstorm with the students some possible categories—grades, hobbies, athletic skills, jobs they've had, other skills—they could use in creating resumés for themselves. List these on chalkboard.
2. Tell students to think of a job they'd like to have. Have them create resumés listing their past accomplishments, strengths, special skills they have which will help them in applying for that job. Tell them they'll have 15 minutes to create their resumés, then you will ask for volunteers to role play a job interview.
3. After 15 minutes ask for volunteers, one to be an interviewer or "boss," the other to be a job applicant, using his or her resumé to "sell" him or herself. As time permits, ask for other volunteers to role play.
4. Process. "How did it feel to try to 'sell' yourself on the basis of your resumé?" "Would someone who was an interviewer or 'boss' tell us what you were feeling when you heard what was in the resumé?" "Any other comments anyone would like to make about this activity?"

Note: You may want to collect and post resumés on a wall as a way for students to learn more about each other.

2.33   DEAR T.L.C.

Materials: None.

Time: 30 minutes.

To the Teacher: These letters are to be responded to by students. They are intended as a focus for discussion.

Directions to Teacher:

1. Have students organize into groups of five. Explain that you have received a letter addressed to "Dear T.L.C." seeking advice like a Dear Abby letter. You will read the letter and ask each group to discuss how the group would reply.
2. Enforce a fifteen-minute time limit.
3. In a large group, have each small group report on their response.
4. Process learning: "In discussing the letter I learned . . ." Have each student either complete the stem or pass.

Letter 1:

"Dear T.L.C.,
  I'm 13 years old and I don't know who I am or what I want to do, so I just go sit in class and go

home and watch TV. I don't know how to get me to do other things—can you help me?"

Signed,
Sitter

Letter 2:

"Dear T.L.C.,

I like me a whole lot. I'm in several clubs, get good grades and am a good student. However, my friends say I don't know how to have a good time. How does one know when to have a good time and when to be serious?"

Signed,
Serious Always

Letter 3:

"Dear T.L.C.,

I like me, but no one has said a good/kind thing to me in weeks. What's wrong?"

Signed,
Lonely

2.34 POETRY/MUSIC "SELF EXPRESSION"

Materials: Record player.

Time: 25 minutes.

To the Teacher: Periodically, and as students want to, a time can be set aside for self expression.

Directions to Teacher:

1. Before this session, encourage students several times to bring poetry and music which says something about them.
2. Have students sit in a large circle and explain that after someone shares their poetry or music, the group will discuss briefly (2–3 minutes) what the presentation was saying.
3. At the end of the session, ask students to complete: "Something I learned today about myself was _____."

3

Communicating

3.1 DICHOTOMIES

Materials: None.

Time: 5 minutes.

To the Teacher: The purpose of "Dichotomies" is to help students think about themselves and their values. As an initial activity in a session, "Dichotomies" serves as an icebreaker. Use only 3–4 dichotomies which are relevant to the day's session.

Directions to Teacher:

1. Create a large open area for students to move about.
2. Explain to students that you will give them a set of words. Each end of the space represents one of the words. When you say the set of words, ask them to move from room center to the end that represents the word with which they identify.
3. Give students an example.

   Step 1
   Students center

   Step 2
   Give choices

                   Students
  (Are you HOT . . . move to   . . . or COLD)
               either end

   Step 3
   Students move
   HOT   COLD

Step 4
Ask students to notice what their choices were, who made the same choice and to share with one other person why they made this choice.

Possible Dichotomies for COMMUNICATING

Talker	or	Listener
Speaker		Preacher
Screamer		Whisperer
Listener		Ignorer
Reaching		Withdrawing
Attending		Preoccupied
Looker		Avoider
Accepting		Rejecting
They		We
Many worded		Few worded
Feeler		Facter
Verbal		Nonverbal

3.2 STEMS

Materials: None.

Time: 10 minutes per stem.

To the Teacher: The purpose of "Stems" is to structure positive responses using sentence stems. Any student should be allowed to pass. Use only one stem per session. Choose one which is relevant to the day's session.

Directions to Teacher:

1. Ask students to form a circle with you.
2. Explain that you are going to start a sentence and you would like for each student in turn to complete it. If a student chooses to pass, make passing acceptable.
3. Give an example by saying the sentence stem, then repeat the sentence stem and complete it yourself. (Your completion will model for the students.)
4. In a structured way (left to right) ask each student to say the start of the sentence (important!) and to complete it.
   > Examples:
   > Teacher (stem) "I feel good when . . ."
   > Teacher (completion) "I feel good when people say positive things to me."
   > Student "I feel good when. . ." (Ask to complete)
   > Student "I feel good when I go home."

Stems

A time when I listened well was _____.

When I know I've been heard I feel _____.

A time when talking something over helped was

_____.

I know other people are listening when they_____

_____.

A time I communicated without words was_____

_____.

Talking with someone older makes me feel_____

_____.

When a baby cries I know _____.

When someone shouts I _____.

3.3 SAYINGS

Materials: None.

Time: 20 minutes.

To the Teacher: The purpose of "Sayings" is to have students examine some famous and not so famous sayings, and discuss the meanings of those sayings to see if they have application in their lives.

Directions to Teacher:

1. Have students sit together in groups of five.
2. Give each group a saying from the list below or write it on the board. Have one student in each group read the statement to his/her group. Small groups discuss what the saying means and how it might apply to them as individuals. PRACTICE LISTENING AND RESPONDING SKILLS.
3. After 15 minutes, get students back into a large group, seated in a circle.
4. Process. "Would any of the groups like to report what you decided the statement means?" "Did another group find some other meaning?" "Would someone like to share what this statement says to him or her?"

Sayings-Communicating

"Speak kind words and you will hear kind echoes."

"It is with narrow-souled people as with narrow-necked bottles: the less they have in them, the more noise they make in pouring it out."

"It is not well for a man to pray cream and live skim milk."

"Nothing makes one feel so strong as a call for help."

"Noise proves nothing. Often a hen who has merely laid an egg cackles as if she had laid an asteroid."

"To reply to a nasty remark with another nasty remark is like trying to remove dirt with mud."

"What you are shouts so loud I cannot hear what you say."

"The water is shallowest where it babbles."

"Let your speech be better than silence or be silent."

"All people smile in the same language."

"Behold the turtle! He only makes progress when he sticks his neck out."

"The silent man is often worth listening to."

"Don't put your mouth in motion before your mind is in gear."

3.4 BRAINSTORMING

Materials: Sheet of paper and pencil for each group.

Time: 15 minutes.

To the Teacher: The purpose of this activity is to encourage students to think of and list as many meanings of the word "COMMUNICATE" as they can so they don't get locked into simply one definition.

Directions to Teacher:

1. Get students into groups of five and have them select a recorder. Give paper and pencil to recorder.
2. Remind students of the rules of brainstorming:
   a. Quantity, not quality, is important.
   b. No discussion or judgments.
   c. Free-wheel, add onto each other's ideas.
3. Tell recorders to write "COMMUNICATE" at the top of their papers.
4. Tell students they have three minutes to think of as many meanings as they can for "COMMUNICATE."
5. Stop after three minutes. Ask each group to

report on the number of ideas they came up with and to share a couple with everyone. (Praise creativity and productiveness.)

6. Bring students back into a large circle to process. "Did you feel good about your contribution to your group's list?" "Are there any new ways you think now about "COMMUNICATION" that you'd like to share with us?"

3.5 DISCUSSION TOPICS

Materials: None.

Time: 20 minutes.

To the Teacher: For teachers and students who like a discussion format, the topics related to this section will serve as a basis for structuring learning through discussion.

Directions to Teacher:

1. Have students sit in one large circle with you.
2. Explain that you would like to have a discussion. The discussion has no ending. There are no "right" or "wrong" answers. Remind students of the rules for group discussion, especially that only one person talks at a time so that everyone can be heard.
3. Introduce the topic and facilitate group interaction.
4. At the end of the discussion ask for someone to summarize the discussion.
5. Process. "One way this discussion was of value to me was _____."

Discussion Topics:

1. "What do we mean when we say 'communications'? Do we need to communicate? What are all the ways we communicate?"
2. "How do you feel when you're talking and no one is listening? Is it important to listen?"
3. "People sometimes say, 'Give me straight talk.' Why would people have to say this?"
4. "How do people communicate nonverbally? Do we need to listen to nonverbal communications?"

3.6 INNER-OUTER DISCUSSION

Materials: None.

Time: 15-20 minutes.

To the Teacher: This activity will help students think about the ways they communicate with others and the effectiveness of their own communications.

Directions to Teacher:

1. Have students number off by 2's. Have all ones make a tight circle. Then have all twos make a circle outside the circle of ones. Tell the inner circle that you're going to ask them to discuss with each other the question, "How do I honestly communicate with myself?" Emphasize honesty. Tell the outer circle that they're to sit very silently and listen. Each of them might pick just one person to watch and listen to. They will get a chance in three minutes to become the inner circle and show how well they listened by repeating what the inner circle people said.
2. Tell the inner circle to begin. "Remember, the question is, 'How do I honestly communicate with myself?'"
3. After three minutes, ask the inner and outer circle members to exchange positions. "Now, inner circle, show you were really listening by repeating what they said." After one minute, say: "Inner circle, now it's your turn. I want you to discuss for three minutes 'How do I honestly communicate with my friends?' Begin now, and outer circle listen only."
4. After three minutes, have the groups change again. Have the new inner circle spend one minute repeating what they heard. Then say, "Now you have three minutes to answer the question 'How do I honestly communicate with my teachers?'"
5. After three minutes, have the groups change once more. Give the new inner circle one minute to repeat what they heard from the former inner circle. Then say, "Now, inner circle, you have three minutes to discuss with each other how you honestly communicate with your parents."
6. Have the inner circle join the outer circle, so they are in one large circle to process. "Would anyone like to share anything he or she learned about communications?" "Did anyone communicate differently with different people or see some changes you need to work on?"

3.7 NAME GAME

Materials: None.

Time: 20-30 minutes.

To the Teacher: Although a group of students may be together regularly, they often don't know each others' names. In a group it is important members refer to each other by name, giving people identities.

Directions to Teacher:

1. Have students sit in a large circle with you.
2. Explain by starting with the student to your left that you'd like each student to share his or her name and favorite food. The catch is that before

you can say your own name and favorite food, you must say the name and food of everyone who's already introduced themselves and their foods. (Teacher will go last, so listen! This is also good because it shows students that you aren't afraid to laugh and make mistakes. This will make you seem more human.)

Note: You may want to repeat this activity later to help students learn names. Other things you might use are name and:

> hobby
> color
> place
> time
> song
> etc.

3.8 PURSE AND WALLET

Materials: None.

Time: 10–15 minutes in groups of five.

To the Teacher: The purpose of this activity is to get students to share something from their purses/wallets/pockets and, in sharing the things, share a little of themselves.

Directions to the Teacher:

1. Ask students to divide into groups of five. Suggest they get with students they do not already know well.
2. After they are in groups explain that you would like them to find something in their purses/wallets/pockets that tells something about them and share it with their group, explaining what the item is and why they chose it.
3. Teacher should model sharing something (the openness of the teacher's sharing will set the model for student sharing).
4. Ask each student to share, spending no more than one minute each.
5. After everyone has shared in his or her group of five, move back into a large group.
6. In the large group, ask students how they felt about their group before they began and after the sharing.

Students should sense some minimal increase in closeness and groupness after the sharing.

3.9 FAMOUS NAMES

Materials: Name tags (1 per student) with a famous person's name on it (list follows).

Time: 10–20 minutes.

To the Teacher: The purpose of this activity is to

get students mixing, and in a structured, non-threatening atmosphere, talking to each other through sharing in a common experience.

Directions to Teacher:

1. Before the session, make the following sign on a big sheet of paper and post it.
   STUDENTS: As you enter, see the teacher to get a famous name. The name will be put on your back. Your objective is to find out who you are. You may ask anyone only two questions that can only be answered yes or no! (Good luck!)
2. As students enter have them read the sign and put names on their backs. (Monitor, in a light-hearted way, for two questions only to any person and yes or no responses.) Allow the game to continue until most students know who they are, but allow no more than 20 minutes.
3. Process. "Did the Famous Names help you talk to many people?" "Will talking to many people help our group?"

Possible Famous Names

Cheryl Tiegs	Benji
Barbra Streisand	Willie Nelson
Snow White	George Jefferson
Mickey Mouse	Waylon Jennings
Big Bird	Archie Bunker
Ronald Reagan	Mr. Spock
Santa Claus	Mick Jagger
Earl Campbell	Tammy Wynette
Mork	Aretha Franklin
Billy Graham	Johnny Rodriquez
Reggie Jackson	Loretta Lynn
Mindy	Wonder Woman
Miss America	Robin Hood
The Fonz	Nancy Drew
Howard Cosell	Diana Ross
Danny White	Darth Vader
Tony Dorsett	Quincy
Evil Knievel	John Travolta
Superman	Adana
Buck Rogers	Snoopy
Dan Rather	Jimmy Connors
Michael Jackson	Jack Nicklaus

3.10 PROVERBS

Materials: Copies of master 3.10, "Proverbs", cut up to allow a half proverb for each student.

Time: 5–15 minutes.

To the Teacher: The purpose of this activity is to get students mixing well with each other.

Directions to Teacher:

1. Before the session, prepare proverbs. Duplicate master 3.10 and cut as shown.
2. Arrange room so there is a large open space.
3. When students are seated, explain that you are going to give each student part of a famous saying and their task in the next 10 minutes will be to find the other half of their famous saying.
4. Give an example of a saying:

    Student 1 would have "A bird in the hand"

    and

    Student 2 would have "is worth two in a bush."
5. Give out sayings, sit back and enjoy.
6. At end of time, ask any pairs to share their saying with the whole group.
7. In a large group discuss. "What is your saying trying to tell us?"

3.11   ROLE PLAY

Materials: Duplicate one copy of master 3.11, role play description, for demonstrators.

Time: 30 minutes.

To the Teacher: The purpose of role playing is to allow students a safe arena where they can try on new behaviors in order to see what they feel like. In the following three role plays, students will watch and discuss alternative ways of communicating with other people.

Directions to Teacher:

1. Before the session, arrange chairs in groups of six. Arrange the groups of six so they can watch a role play.
2. When students are seated, explain that they are going to watch a communications role play. After the role play, each group is to decide on an alternative way of handling the situation.
3. Ask for two volunteers and give each his or her role sheet. Do not tell the class their roles.
4. After the demonstration, ask for a student to explain the situation as he or she saw it. Continue the discussion until you get an accurate situation described.
5. Give the groups 10 minutes to prepare an alternative.
6. After 10 minutes, call time and have groups share their alternatives through role play demonstrations.
7. After presentations, in a large group, process. "What I learned in this exercise about communications is _____."

3.12   START A SOUND

Materials: None.

Time: 10 minutes.

To the Teacher: This activity will help students learn to listen and then communicate what they heard.

Directions to Teacher:

1. Have students seated in one large circle with you.
2. One student starts a sound. The person next to him picks it up and repeats it with him until he can duplicate it exactly. Then he alone keeps the sound until he transforms it into a sound of his own. The next person picks up that sound, imitates it, makes it his own, then passes it on to the next. Continue around the circle.
3. After the sound has gone around the circle, process. "How did it feel, trying to make someone else's sound all alone by yourself?"

3.13   ORCHESTRA

Materials: None.

Time: 10 minutes.

To the Teacher: This will help students learn to communicate through rhythm, with their bodies, and with sounds other than words.

Directions to Teacher:

1. Split class into two groups.
2. Let each group choose a conductor and have them sit in a semi-circle, conductor facing them.
3. Everyone is to create a sound (not words) or rhythm, using voice (not too loud!), hands, feet, etc. The group conductor leads them in rehearsal.
4. After five minutes of rehearsal, let groups perform for each other.
5. In a large circle, process. "What did you learn about communicating in this way?"

3.14   ONE WAY/TWO WAY COMMUNICATION

Materials: Paper and pencil for each student.

Time: 30 minutes.

To the Teacher: The purpose of this activity is to let students see the importance of audio and visual feedback in communication and the uses of defining terms and identifying reference points.

Directions to Teacher:

1. Study the series of squares in figure 3.14A.

2. Explain to the class what is going to happen; that they are to draw what is described without questions.
3. With your back to the class, you are to direct the students in how they are to draw the figures. Begin with the top square and describe each in succession, taking particular note of the relationship of each to the preceding one. NO QUESTIONS ARE ALLOWED.

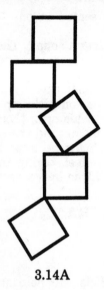

3.14A

4. When the description is complete, put the described diagram on the board to compare results.
5. In a large circle discuss: "How did you feel, not being allowed to ask questions as you worked?"
6. Select another student to study the series of squares in figure 3.14B.

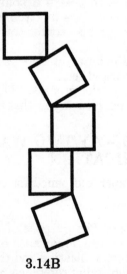

3.14B

7. Explain to the class that this time they are to draw what is described and they may ask questions.

8. Facing the class you are to direct the students in how to draw the figures. Begin with the top square and describe each in succession, taking particular note of the relation of each to the preceding one. ANSWER ALL QUESTIONS FROM STUDENTS AND REPEAT IF NECESSARY.
9. When the description is complete, draw the diagram on the board.
10. In a large circle, process. "What are the advantages of two way communications?" "How did you feel, being allowed to ask questions?"

3.15 ACCIDENT REPORT

Materials: Copy of master 3.15, Accident Report Sheet, and a pencil for each student, cassette recorder if possible.

Time: 20 minutes.

To the Teacher: The purpose of this activity is that students will learn difficulties in transferring information accurately and will want to improve their skills in this area.

Directions to Teacher:

1. Ask for six volunteers to play the report chain. Give them numbers one through six and send them out of the room.
2. Give each of the remaining students an Accident Report Work Sheet. Read over the Accident Report with the class and explain that you will call in the first member of the report chain and read him or her the accident report. The first member will then call in the second member of the report chain and will retell the report to the best of his or her ability. Then the second member will call in the third, and so on until all have been called in and hear the report from the person just ahead of him or her on the report chain. (You may wish to record all the repetitions.)
3. As each member reports to the next on the chain, the rest of the class is to note any changes in the new version from the previous report on the blanks on the work sheet.
4. As soon as the sixth member of the report chain repeats the accident report to the teacher and class, the teacher reads the initial report once more.
5. Discuss with students the difficulties in transferring information accurately, the reactions of the six members of the reporting chain, and their feelings as they tried to concentrate on the message.

3.16 GROUP STORY

Materials: None.

Time: 10–15 minutes.

To the Teacher: This activity will help students learn to listen closely to each other.

Directions to Teacher:

1. Ask students to get into groups of seven or eight to work on a group story.
2. The students should sit in a circle, close together so they can hear each other easily. Anyone who wishes may start the story and others contribute to the story with individuals spontaneously taking over. The rest of the group will go along, as if it were their story, with whoever is describing what is happening in the story at that time.
3. After ten minutes, get the students back into a large group and process. "Did you learn anything about yourself you'd like to share, either as a listener or a story teller?"

3.17 COMMUNICATING GOODBYE

Materials: None.

Time: 15–20 minutes.

To the Teacher: This will enable students to think about their closest friends, who they are, how they feel about them, how open they can allow themselves to be with them.

Directions to Teacher:

1. Have students get into groups of five.
2. Say: "The four others in your group are your best, closest friends. You may re-name them, if you like, if it will make it easier to let them represent the people who really are the four friends you are closest to. You have just been told this morning at breakfast that your dad is being transferred, that in one week you are moving away. Think about these friends, what they mean to you, how it will be to leave them. Then one by one, say goodbye to each person in your group. Role play leaving them. Say goodbye the way you really feel. One person in each group will begin by saying goodbye to each of the four people in his or her group who represent his or her closest friends."
3. After fifteen minutes, have everyone get into a large group to process. "Were you able to really say goodbye the way you felt?" "What did you learn about yourself?"

3.18 FEEDBACK TRIADS

Materials: None.

Time: 30 minutes.

To the Teacher: The purpose of this activity is to help students listen and to give accurate feedback.

Directions to Teacher:

1. Have students group in sets of three. Have group members letter themselves A, B, C.
2. Explain that one important skill needed for good group working is listening and giving feedback. The intent of this exercise is to help us practice listening and feedback. Each student in turn will have three minutes to talk about a topic. At the end of three minutes, one student will summarize what was said. The third student will verify the feedback.

   > A = 1st talker
   > B = 1st listener/summarizer
   > C = 1st verifier

   Topic: Things I Like Doing With My Friends.
3. At the end of three minutes ask B to take one minute to feedback what A said. Then ask C to say if feedback was "on target."
4. Repeat   B = talker
                  C = listener
                  A = verifier
5. Repeat   C = talker
                  A = listener
                  B = verifier
6. After the three rounds, in a large circle process. "How did you feel when you were listener?" "How did you feel as talker when you got on-target feedback?" "What things can we do to show we're listening?"

3.19 BODY LANGUAGE AWARENESS

Materials: TV set.

Time: 10–15 minutes.

To the Teacher: The purpose of this activity is to try to see what is expressed non-verbally by gestures, posture and body positions.

Directions to Teacher:

1. Turn the television set on to a picture showing a close-up of actors. Turn the sound off.
2. Ask the class to spend two minutes observing all of the gestures and body positions which carry communication.
3. After two minutes turn the picture off and hold a general discussion of what they noticed.

4. Repeat this procedure several times, finding close-up and long shots, as each new viewing will reveal new insights into body language.
5. In a large group process. "What did you discover today about body language?"

3.20 SILENT MIRROR

Materials: None.

Time: 10–15 minutes.

To the Teacher: This activity will help students learn to communicate non-verbally with each other.

Directions to Teacher:
1. Have students pair off and go to a place in the room where they have some space around them.
2. Each pair should decide who is the leader and who is the mirror. They stand facing each other at about an arm's length, feet apart, eyes on the floor. The leader moves his or her eyes slowly across the other person until they make eye contact. The leader initiates movement very slowly while the partner mirrors that movement exactly. Keep eye contact throughout. When "switch" is called let the partner continue the movement. Keep eye contact. Rely on peripheral vision to follow the body movement. As students become skillful at changing back from one role to another, they may be able to synchronize movements so there is no leader and no follower.
3. In a large group process. "What did you discover about yourself and your 'mirror'"?

3.21 I SEE, THEREFORE I PRESUME

Materials: None.

Time: 15 minutes.

To the Teacher: This activity will allow students to see what they communicate non-verbally to others and will help them see the mistakes which are sometimes the result of first impressions.

Directions to Teacher:
1. Have students pair off into twos and have each pair sit facing each other.
2. One person makes the statements and the other can answer only yes or no. The person making the statements begins each with the phrase: "I see _____, therefore I presume that _____." For example, "I see you're wearing glasses, therefore I presume you are nearsighted." This goes on for three minutes and then the roles are reversed.
3. Pairs talk afterwards about the mistakes, pre-

sumptions, etc. they made in looking at each other.
4. Process. "Would someone like to share something he or she learned from this activity?"

3.22 DEAR T.L.C.

Materials: None.

Time: 30 minutes.

To the Teacher: These letters are to be responded to by students. They are intended as focus for discussion.

Directions to Teacher:
1. Have students organize into groups of five. Explain that you have received a letter addressed to "Dear T.L.C." seeking advice like a Dear Abby letter. You will read the letter and ask each group to discuss how the group would reply.
2. Enforce a fifteen minute time limit.
3. In a large group, have each small group report on its response.
4. Process. "In discussing the letter, I learned . . ." (Have each student, in turn, complete stem or pass.)

Letter 1
Dear T.L.C.,
    I'm writing you this letter because I want to tell someone I really like her as a person but every time I try to say it, I just freeze up. How can I say "I like you" without words?
                                            Signed,
                                            Speechless

Letter 2
Dear T.L.C.,
    I have this teacher who is always smiling while she yells at us. I don't know why I feel like she isn't being honest but that's how I feel. What do you say to that?
                                            Signed,
                                            Double-Messaged

Letter 3
Dear T.L.C.,
    It seems that lately every time I get angry I go off in a corner and pout. I don't like to be alone and pout. My friends say I should learn other ways to deal with my anger. Can you suggest how I can deal with my anger?
                                            Signed,
                                            Ex-Pouter

3.23 POETRY/MUSIC "SELF EXPRESSION"

Materials: Record player.

Time: 25 minutes.

To the Teacher: Periodically, and as students want to, a time can be set aside for self expression.

Directions to Teacher:

1. Before this session, encourage students several times to bring poetry and music which says something about the art of communications.
2. Have students sit in a large circle and explain that after someone shares their poetry or music, the group will discuss briefly (2–3 minutes) what the presentation was saying.
3. At the end of the session, ask students to complete: "Something I learned about communications today was . . ."

4

Building Groups

4.1 DISCUSSION OF RULES FOR GROUP

Materials: None.

Time: 30 minutes (if closure is not obtained, a second session should follow).

To the Teacher: Sometimes it is important for a group to sit down and, through a series of questions, discuss issues critical to the group. This question set is designed to help a group set rules for itself. It is not necessary to use these questions like a cookbook, it is the direction in which the questions take students which is of value.

Directions to Teacher:

1. Have students sit in a circle with you.
2. Make one request for this discussion, that being that people listen and not interrupt each other.
3. Discussion questions:
   a. "How do you feel when someone takes something of yours?" (Students will say it makes them feel bad, angry, sad, etc. Make sure everyone who wants to respond to the question gets the opportunity to do so, but does not feel forced to do so.)
   b. "What keeps people from taking things from other people?" (Students will mention rules, fear of retaliation, laws, etc.)

c. "What would happen if we had no rules or laws?" (Bedlam, chaos, no rights, couldn't keep anything.)
d. "Would not having laws/rules make any difference?" (Students make value judgments, hopefully, deciding rules as necessary.)
e. "If we say we need rules to protect our individual rights, what rules should we have in here?" (Students and teacher develop a set of rules all can live with. Rules should be few and simple. For Example:
   1. One talks at a time
   2. Speak about self, not others
   3. Respect someone's right to remain silent
   4. What is said in the group remains in the group.

4.2 STYLE SHOW

Materials: Large stacks of newspapers and one box of flat toothpicks for each group.

Time: 25 minutes.

To the Teacher: The purpose of this activity is team building and problem solving. You might want to observe for yourself, or process in a large group, the various roles students assumed.

Directions to the Teacher:

1. Get students into groups of 7 or 8. Give each group a large stack of newspapers and a box of toothpicks.
2. Tell students they have 15 minutes to select one person from each group to be their "model" for a style show. It is the task of the other group members to create a costume on that person, using only the newspapers and toothpicks. They should strive for as complete and creative a costume as possible.
3. After 15 minutes, get students back into large circle. Have the models stand in the center, turn slowly and show off their group's "creation." Have judges if possible.
4. Process. "Did you learn something about yourself as a group member?" "Who of you automatically became designers?" "Who became models?" "How did you feel about your participation in this activity?"

4.3 WANT AD
(Note: Follow with 4.4 "CLASSIFIED AD")

Materials: Paper and pencil for each group.

Time: 20 minutes.

To the Teacher: This activity will enable students to think about what sort of person contributes most to a group. It should be used with groups who have spent enough time together that they trust each other and already have a sense of cohesiveness.

Directions to Teacher:

1. Have students get into groups of five and have each small group choose a recorder. Give paper and pencil to recorder.
2. Tell students: "Each of your groups has five members. I want you to think about your group, about how you feel about each other, about the sort of people you five are and are trying to become. Then imagine that you have been told that each group will be enlarged by adding one more student. Think about what kind of person you would like to join your group. Also think about what your group has to offer a prospective member. Think about it silently for a couple of minutes, then discuss it among yourselves and compose a "Want Ad" to advertise for the sort of person you would like in your group. Have your recorder write out the "Want Ad" for your group, then we will all get together in the large

group and share our ads. You have ten minutes, so begin thinking silently now."
3. Have students get back into a large circle. Have recorder or another student from each group read their "Want Ad" to the large group.
4. Process. "Did you think of any new group goals as you tackled this problem?" "Would anyone like to share yours with us?" "Did any of you as individuals learn something new about yourself which you would be willing to tell us now?"

4.4 CLASSIFIED AD
(Note: Do 4.3 "WANT AD" first)

Materials: Paper and pencil for each group.

Time: 20 minutes.

To the Teacher: The purpose of this activity is to have students think about their small groups, the strengths they have both as individuals and as a group, and be able to "sell" to the large group.

Directions to Teacher:

1. Have students get in the same groups of five as at previous T L C meeting time. Ask them to choose a recorder and give paper and pencil to recorder.
2. Tell students: "Your groups have met together several times. By this time, you should be fairly well aware of your own individual strengths, your group's positive characteristics and the purpose behind all our T L C activities. Think silently about these things, then after a couple of minutes discuss them with each other. What I want you to do is come up with a classified advertisement which begins: 'Group Available who . . .' Recorders, you write down the classified ad for your group and remember to begin it with 'Group Available who . . .' You have ten minutes, so begin now thinking to yourselves what kind of group you are."
3. Have everyone get into a large circle. The recorder, or someone else chosen by the small group, will read their ad to the large group. After all small groups have read their classified ads, process. "Would any group like to share any new strengths you found in your group as you discussed your ad?" "Anyone else?" "Would anyone like to respond to any group's ad?" "Would this group's ad appeal to you or make you want to hire them?"

4.5 STRENGTHS BOMBARDMENT

Materials: Pencils, five 3 x 5 index cards per person.

Time: 15 minutes.

To the Teacher: The purpose of "Strengths Bombardment" is to make students more comfortable with giving and receiving positive feedback and to help them identify strengths in themselves and others.

Directions to Teacher:

1. Divide the entire group into groups of five and give each student five 3×5 index cards.
2. Ask each student to write at the tops of the five cards the names of the five people in his or her group, including himself or herself (one name on each card).
3. Ask students to write on each card, below the name on the card, four good things about that person, including himself or herself.
4. After students have finished writing, go in turn around the group, focusing on one individual while each person reads his or her list of good things about that person, then give that person the cards. Then move on and focus on the next person in the group until each person has been the subject of a "strengths bombardment" and has collected all his or her cards. (Stress the importance of *MEANING* what you say and of receiving "gifts" (positive feedback) graciously).
5. Process. Get students back in a large circle. Ask if they would like to share how they felt about giving and/or receiving positive feedback. Do they feel differently now than when they first came into the room? How?

4.6 BRAGGING

Materials: None.

Time: 20–30 minutes.

To the Teacher: The purpose of this activity is to encourage students to feel good about themselves and to build group rapport. It is important to receive recognition and support from others.

Directions to Teacher:

1. Have students sitting together in small groups of 5 or 6 members.
2. Say, "Each of you has 3 minutes to brag about yourself to the others in your group. Think about what you really like about yourself, maybe something no one else knows about you. But it can be anything—personal characteristics, skills you have, awards, things you do well. No one will put you down for bragging."
3. After everyone has bragged, form one large group and process. "How did you feel about

bragging on yourself?" "How was it to listen to others brag about themselves?"

4.7 SELFING

Materials: None.

Time: 10 minutes.

To the Teacher: The purpose of this activity is to provide a safe controlled way students can share who they are.

Directions to Teacher:

1. Ask students to get in groups of six.
2. Ask students to spend 2 minutes quietly thinking of 6 words that end in "ing" that describe them.
3. Model for students describing yourself with "ing" words—i.e., leading, loving, golfing, eating, etc.
4. Ask students to share their 6 words with their group.
5. Process. "What did you learn from selfing—describing yourself using "ing" words?"

Variations: You can use the same process with nouns, adjectives, etc.

4.8 ALL THINGS WRONG

Materials: Sheet of paper and pencil for each group.

Time: 20–30 minutes.

To the Teacher: This activity demonstrates how much easier it is to be negative than positive.

Directions to Teacher:

1. Ask students to get in groups of 6 and select a member to be recorder of ideas.
2. Have each recorder get a sheet of paper and pencil and divide the paper into 2 columns.
3. Tell the groups they will have 5 minutes to generate a list of as many things wrong with a *bathtub* as possible.

Note: Other items: swing, bottle, plane, desk, candle.

4. After 5 minutes have them stop and spend the next 5 minutes generating a list of all things *right* with a *bathtub*.
5. Stop after 5 minutes and process. "Was it easier to be positive or negative? Why?" "How does this activity apply to productive working groups?"

4.9 TRULY YOU

Materials: None.

Time: 20–30 minutes.

To the Teacher: This is a movement activity which helps students see how they are alike and different. It enables students to share self as a basis for building trust. This is an especially appropriate activity for non-talkative groups.

Directions to Teacher:

1. Ask students to move furniture so there is a wide open space.
2. Ask students to stand in the middle.
3. Explain that one end of the space represents "Truly Like You" and the other end is "Unlike You." You will make a statement and students are to move to a place between the two ends that is them.
4. Do an example:

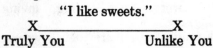

"I like sweets."

X_____X

Truly You   Unlike You

Ask students to move to the point that represents them.

5. After the exercise, form a large group and process. "What did you learn about others in this exercise?" "What did you learn about yourself?"

"Truly You" Statements

I have fun.
Everyday is a new day.
I accept other points of view.
I like me.
I like surprises.
I enjoy people.
I like alone time.
I believe in planning before action.
My life has purpose.
I control my temper.
I am never bored.
People are important.
I respect others.
I exercise regularly.
I am patient.
I judge others by their clothes.
I choose how I feel.

4.10 STRENGTHS TARGET

Materials: One Strengths Target for each student.

Time: 15 minutes.

To the Teacher: This activity will help students identify and share the strengths they bring to the group and areas where they will look to other group members' strengths.

Directions to Teacher:

1. As a large group generate a list of strengths different persons bring to a group (list where all can see).

   e.g., creativity.
        clarifier.
        summarizer.

2. Hand out a Strengths Target to each student and ask them to individually list in the center of the target the one greatest strength they bring to the group.
3. After a few minutes, ask them in the outer ring of the target to list other strengths they bring to the group.
4. After a few minutes, ask them to list outside the target areas where they look to other group members' strengths.
5. After a few minutes, ask them to share with their small group and identify the greatest strength of the group and the area where the group may need the most help.
6. Share with the entire class their group strengths and help areas.
7. Process as a total group. "What does this exercise say about individuals and a group?"

4.11 HOLLOW SQUARE

Materials: A set of envelopes containing pieces of the square for each group of students. Prepare square according to diagram in figure 4.11.

Time: 30 minutes.

To the Teacher: The purpose of this exercise is to demonstrate that each member of the group must contribute if the group is to be successful.

Directions to Teacher:

1. Before the class prepare a set of envelopes, with pieces of the hollow square, for each group (see figure 4.11).
2. Ask students to get into groups of five.
3. Hand out a set of envelopes to each group and explain that there are pieces of a hollow square in each envelope. It is the job of the group to build a hollow square. The rules are:
   1. No talking.
   2. You can only use your pieces (do not touch anyone else's).
4. Begin.
5. Stop after most are complete and process. "What does this activity say about cooperation in groups?" "What would happen to a group if one member withheld his pieces (info)?"

HOLLOW SQUARE PATTERN

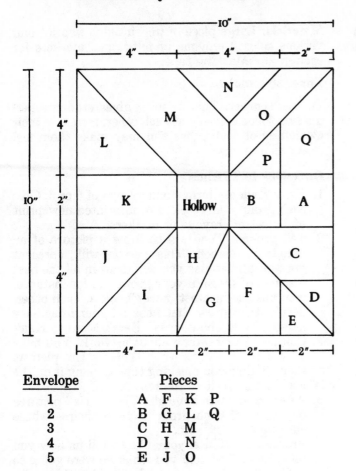

Envelope	Pieces			
1	A	F	K	P
2	B	G	L	Q
3	C	H	M	
4	D	I	N	
5	E	J	O	

4.12 FIVE SQUARES

Materials: A set of 5 envelopes with appropriate pieces for each 5-member group. Prepare squares according to diagram in figure 4.12.

Time: 30 minutes.

To the Teacher: The purpose of this exercise is to show students that all members of a group must cooperate for the group to be successful.

Directions to Teacher:

1. Before class prepare a "5 squares" set for each group of 5 students.
2. Ask students to get seated in groups of 5 with a common work space (desks, floor, table).
3. Hand out envelope set to each student and tell students not to open envelopes.
4. Explain that there are pieces of 5 squares in each envelope. It is the job of the group to build 5 equal sized squares—one in front of each group member. The rules are:

1. No talking.
2. You cannot take; only give.
3. No signals.

5. Tell them to begin.
6. When most groups are done or after 15 minutes stop the activity and process. "What did this activity teach you about groups completing group tasks?" "What does this activity say about cooperation in groups?"

5 SQUARES

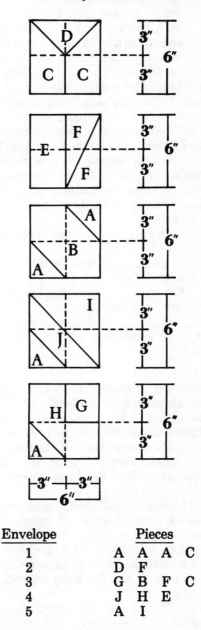

Envelope	Pieces			
1	A	A	A	C
2	D	F		
3	G	B	F	C
4	J	H	E	
5	A	I		

Note: Each square is 6″ × 6″.

4.13 TRIVIA SHEET

Materials: "Trivia Sheet" and a pencil for each participant. Note: Trivia Sheets are created in part I of this activity.

Time: 20–30 minutes.

To the Teacher: This activity enables students to share with each other little-known facts about themselves.

Directions to Teacher: This activity has two parts.
Part I:
1. At the end of a class period or day assign students the following task: "Tomorrow I want each of you to turn in to me a sheet of paper on which you've written some bit of information about yourself which no one else knows. It can be anything you might want to share about yourself, something which might surprise those who know you. For example, were you born in a taxi cab? Did you win a "Most Beautiful Baby" contest? Were you an angel in the Christmas play at church? Write down something about yourself and turn it in to me tomorrow." (If you like you might let them simply tell you what it is and you write it down. But be sure no one else hears or sees it!)
2. Next put all this on a dittoed sheet like a test. *Example:*
   1. _____ was born in the back seat of the family car.
   2. _____ My mother was a "Miss America" contestant.
   3. _____ I have a dog who wakes me up each morning when my mom tells him to.

Part II:
1. Students are in groups of 10 to 12. Hand out a dittoed sheet to each student.
2. Announce that this "Trivia Sheet" contains all the information they turned in about themselves. They are to work in their small groups, write in all the names of their classmates whom they can identify. They have 15 minutes to do this.
3. After 15 minutes, call time. Leader explains that now we shall see which small group got the most correct answers. Read the first bit of trivia, ask whom that describes. If no one knows, ask the person who turned it in to raise his or her hand. Then go to next one. Continue until all people are identified.
4. Process. "Did anyone learn anything about yourself which you'd like to share?" "How was it, letting your small group know that was you?"

4.14 THIS IS US

Materials: Large piece of unprinted newsprint and various colored crayons or felt-tipped markers for each group. Masking tape.

Time: 30 minutes.

To the Teacher: This activity gives students permission to look closely at each other, increases their awareness of each other and may make them feel closer as a group.

Directions to Teacher:
1. Have students form small groups of 5 or 6. Give each group a large piece of unprinted newsprint and a set of crayons or markers.
2. Tell groups: "You are to draw a picture of an imaginary person. This person will represent your group because you will draw in all the best features of those in your group ... for instance, who has the 'neatest' nose? Look at each other, decide, then draw that nose on your imaginary person. How about eyes? Ears? Mouth? Hair? Clothes? Don't worry about artwork! You have 15 minutes to draw your 'This Is Us' picture, then I'll give you masking tape to hang it on the wall and show it to the rest of us."
3. After 15 minutes have all "This Is Us" pictures on wall. Let each group explain theirs—whose ears were "best," etc.
4. Process. "Would anyone like to tell us how you felt when I first told you what we were going to do?" "How do you feel now?" "Anything else you'd like to share about this activity?"

4.15 BLOCKERS AND BUILDERS

Materials: Duplicate master 4.15, Blockers and Builders. A different role card should be prepared for each member of each group.

Time: 25–30 minutes.

To the Teacher: This activity is to show students what negative behaviors can do to a group.

Directions to Teacher:
1. Ask students to get in groups of eight.
2. Hand out a role card to each student. Tell them not to share their cards with the group. (If you have groups of 7, delete role 5.)
3. Explain that the school has agreed to let them spend a day together doing something outside school, if they can decide in the next 10 minutes how they will spend that day.

4. After 10 minutes, stop the groups and process as a total group. "Were all the group members trying to reach a decision?" "Were there any behaviors which blocked the group in reaching a decision?" "What were the results of the blocking behaviors?"

4.16 TURN ON, TURN OFF

Materials: Duplicate master 4.16, Turn On, Turn Off for each student.

Time: 30 minutes.

To the Teacher: The purpose of this activity is to help groups become aware of words and phrases that keep a group working and words and phrases that cause a group to stop working. (This exercise should only be used by already functioning groups.)

Directions to Teacher:

1. Ask students (already in working groups) to reflect back on times they have worked together, and individually list things which have been said that turned them off and turned them on as a participating group member by filling out the "Turn On, Turn Off" work sheet.
2. Give an example of a turn on and a turn off statement:
   Turn on: "That is a neat idea!"
   Turn off: "We shouldn't do that."
3. Give individuals 5–10 minutes to do their own lists.
4. Ask groups to share their individual turn-ons and turn-offs and build a group list. Allow 10 minutes.
5. Process. "How could your group make use of your turn-on and turn-off list when you're working together?"

4.17 LABELS

Materials: Duplicate master 4.17, labels so there is a label for each student. (Note: There are two different sets of labels.)

Time: 20 minutes (label set 1); 30 minutes (label set 2).

To the Teacher: This activity provides experience with labels that cause students' involvement in a group to be hindered.

Directions to Teacher:

1. Before class prepare a label with tape for each student. (Variation: make head bands with labels on them.)

2. At the start explain that often because of labels people put on us, they limit our participation in a group.
3. Place a label on each student so he/she doesn't know the label he/she is wearing.
4. Ask students to walk around and talk with as many students as possible and respond to the labels, not the people.
5. After 5–10 minutes, depending on the group, stop and process. "How was this experience for you?" "What does this activity tell us about labels we put on people?"

4.18 OUTSIDER/INSIDER

Materials: None.

Time: 30 minutes.

To the Teacher: This activity enables students to get in touch with feelings of being excluded from a group as well as from excluding others.

Directions to Teacher:

1. Have students get into groups of 5 or 6. Ask one member of each group to be the "outsider." Take outsiders aside and "coach" them on breaking-in. They may not use any physical force. They may speak to the members any way they wish. They may try to go under arms, tap on shoulders, anything non-violent.
2. Tell group members that they may not respond verbally to outsiders' pleas or actions. They plan how to keep outsiders out. They may relent and let the outsider in if they think he or she merits membership because of something he or she has said or done.
3. Tell outsiders to try to break in. After 2 minutes, stop them and someone else from each group becomes the outsider. Continue until each group member has been the "outsider."
4. After each has had a turn as outsider, ask all outsiders who did not obtain entry into the group to remain outside of large circle which is made up of all group members.
5. Outsiders all at the same time try to gain entry into the large circle.
6. When all members are admitted into one large group or 10 minutes is up form one circle and process. "How did it feel to be outside the group?" "How did it feel to be inside the group and keeping someone else out?" "Does anyone see any connection between this activity and groups here at school?"

4.19 THE CAR WASH

Materials: None.

Time: 5–10 minutes.

To the Teacher: This activity is designed to build group cohesiveness and enable students to feel good about themselves and each other. It is recommended that not more than one or two people be run through the "car wash" each day so that responses will be fresh, personalized and enthusiastic.

Directions to Teacher:

1. Line up entire class in two parallel lines, close together and all facing forward.

2. Tell students to think of "car wash" places they have seen, how shiny and new-looking even the oldest, most banged-up cars look when they come out. Ask for a volunteer, someone who maybe is feeling "down" or "blah," who'd like to come out all "shiny and new-feeling." Or it may be someone the class decides they'd like to give a good feeling to. Explain that the student will be sent through the "wash" (between the lines) and everyone will touch him or her, with handshakes or pats on the back, and say words of praise or caring or encouragement.

3. Process. " 'Washers,' what would you share about giving that 'car' all that special treatment?" " 'Car,' could you tell us if you felt as new and shiny as you looked when you came out of the car wash?"

5

Relating to Others

5.1 DICHOTOMIES

Materials: None.

Time: 5 minutes.

To the Teacher: The purpose of "Dichotomies" is to help students think about themselves and their values. As an initial activity in a session, "Dichotomies" serves as an icebreaker. Use only 3–4 dichotomies which are relevant to the day's session.

Directions to Teacher:

1. Create a large open area for students to move about.
2. Explain to students that you will give them a set of words. Each end of the space represents one of the words. When you say the set of words, ask them to move from room center to the end that represents the word with which they identify.
3. Give students an example.

   Step 1
   Students center

   Step 2
   Give choices
   Are you HOT . . .   . . . or COLD

   Step 3
   Students move

   Students

HOT   move to   COLD
             either end

Step 4
Ask students to notice what their choice was, who made the same choice and to share with one other person why they made this choice.

Possible Dichotomies for *Relating To Others:*
In relation to other people, am I . . .

selfish	generous
friendly	hostile
open	closed
grabber	receiver
lover	hater
sharing	stingy
taker	giver
close	distant
openminded	closed minded
toucher	stand-off
cold	hot
positive	negative

5.2 STEMS

Materials: None.

Time: 10 minutes per stem.

To the Teacher: The purpose of "Stems" is to structure positive responses using sentence stems.

Any student should be allowed to pass. Use only one stem per session. Choose one which is relevant to the day's session.

Directions to Teacher:

1. Ask students to form a circle with you.
2. Explain that you are going to start a sentence and you would like for each student in turn to complete it. If a student chooses to pass, make passing acceptable.
3. Give an example by saying the sentence stem, then repeat the sentence stem and complete it yourself. (Your completion will model for the students.)
4. In a structured way (left to right) ask each student to say the start of the sentence (important!) and to complete it.
> Examples:
> Teacher (stem) "I feel good when . . ."
> Teacher (completion) "I feel good when people say positive things to me."
> Student "I feel good when. . ." (Ask student to make stem into a full sentence.)
> Student "I feel good when I go home."

Stems

One thing I value in others is _____.
A friend of mine must be _____.
A good friend is one who _____.
Being with people I like makes me feel _____.
When I meet someone I want to know better, I
_____.
I want to be a friend who _____.
I want people to like me because _____.
Having older friends _____.
I like people who _____.
I need other people because _____.
How I would like other people to feel about me is
_____.
A time someone showed he or she liked me was
_____.
When someone tells me something good about me, I
feel _____.
I let someone know I like him or her by _____.
The way I decide I like a person is _____.

5.3 SAYINGS

Materials: None.

Time: 20 minutes.

To the Teacher: The purpose of "SAYINGS" is to have students examine some famous and not-so-

famous sayings, and discuss the meanings of those sayings and see if they have application in their lives.

Directions to Teacher:

1. Have students sit together in groups of five.
2. Give each group a saying from the list below. Have one student in each group read the statement to his/her group. Small groups discuss what the saying means and how it might apply to them as individuals. PRACTICE LISTENING AND RESPONDING SKILLS.
3. After fifteen minutes, get students back into a large group, seated in a circle.
4. Process. "Would any of the groups like to report what they decided the statement means?" "Did another group find some other meaning?" "Would someone like to share what this statement says to him or her?"

Sayings—Relating to Others

"People are lonely because they build walls instead of bridges."
"There is no desert like being friendless."
"No man is an island."
"A friendless man is like a right hand without a left."
"A friend is not a shadow that is present only when the sun shines."
"A torn jacket is soon mended, but hard words bruise the heart of a child."
"Friendship is a creature formed for a companionship, not for a herd."
"Fate makes our relatives; choice makes our friends."
"No man is the whole of himself; his friends are the rest of him."

5.4 BRAINSTORMING

Materials: Sheet of paper and pencil for each group.

Time: 15 minutes.

To the Teacher: The purpose of this activity is to encourage students to think of and list as many meanings of "OTHERS" as they can so they do not get locked into simply one definition.

Directions to Teacher:

1. Get students into groups of five and have them select a recorder. Give paper and pencil to recorder.
2. Remind students of the rules of brainstorming.
   a. Quantity, not quality, is important.
   b. No discussion or judgments.
   c. Free-wheel, add onto each other's ideas.

3. Tell recorders to write "OTHERS" at the top of their papers.
4. Tell students "You have three minutes to think of as many meanings as you can for 'OTHERS'."
5. Stop after three minutes. Ask each group to report on the number of ideas they came up with and to share a couple with everyone. (Praise creativity and productivity.)
6. Bring students back into a large circle to process. "Did you feel good about your contributions to your group's list?" "Are there any new meanings you can think of now about 'OTHERS' that you'd like to share with us?"

5.5 DISCUSSION

Materials: None.

Time: 20 minutes.

To the Teacher: For teachers and students who like a discussion format, the topics related to this section will serve as a basis for structuring learning through discussion.

Directions to Teacher:

1. Have students sit in one large circle with you.
2. Explain that you would like to have a discussion. The discussion has no ending. There is no one right or wrong answer. Remind students of the rules for group discussion, especially that only one person talks at a time so everyone can be heard.
3. Introduce the topic and facilitate group interaction.
4. At the end of the discussion, ask for someone to summarize the discussion.
5. Process. "One way this discussion was of value to me is _____."

Discussion Topics:

1. What is a "friend"?
2. What is trust? How do we get trust? Is it important to trust?
3. How do you make friends?
4. Can family be friends?

5.6 ROLE PLAY

Materials: One copy of master 5.6, Role Play Descriptions, cut up, for demonstrations.

Time: 30 minutes.

To the Teacher: The purpose of role playing is to allow students a safe arena where they can try on new behaviors to see what they feel like. In the following three role plays, the students will watch and discuss alternative ways of interacting with other people.

Directions to Teacher:

1. Before the session, arrange chairs in groups of six. Arrange the groups of six so they can watch a role play.
2. When students are seated, explain that they are going to watch a person-to-person role play. After the role play, each group is to decide on an alternative way of handling the situation.
3. Ask for two volunteers and give each his or her role sheet. Do not tell the class their roles.
4. After the demonstration, ask for a student to explain the situation as he or she saw it. Continue the discussion until you get an accurate situation described.
5. Give the groups ten minutes to prepare an alternative.
6. After ten minutes, call time and have the groups share their alternative.
7. After presentations in a large group, process. "What I learned in this exercise about dealing people-to-people is _____."

5.7 $1000 TO GIVE AWAY

Materials: None.

Time: 10–15 minutes.

To the Teacher: This activity will enable students to think about what or who, outside of themselves, is important to them.

Directions to Teacher:

1. Have students get in a large circle.
2. Say: "Pretend, if you will, that I have suddenly struck oil or something and have been given a huge sum of money. Since you, my T L C group, have come to mean so much to me I am going to share my wealth with you. I am going to give you each ONE THOUSAND DOLLARS! Imagine that! $1,000! The only condition I set as I give each of you the thousand dollars is that you must give it away. You may not keep any of it, nor may you spend any of it on yourself. You *must* spend it or give it away to someone else or some cause. Who would like to begin by telling us what you are going to do with your thousand dollars? Why did you choose to use it that way?" (Let students share with the group, stressing again listening and responding skills.)
3. After seven or eight minutes, process. "How did it feel to give it away or spend it on someone else?" "Did anyone learn something about him-

self or herself as a giver?" "Who else would like to share how you felt about being told you had to spend it on someone or something other than yourself?"

5.8 COMMONALITIES

Materials: None.

Time: 15 minutes.

To the Teacher: The purpose of this activity is to help students see that, in spite of obvious differences, they have many things in common with each other.

Directions to Teacher:

1. Ask students to form a large circle.
2. Ask that all students who have a pet dog enter the center of the circle and walk about at random. Comment on the commonality, that is, they each have a dog. Have them look at each other, see who has this in common with them. Then ask them to return to their places in the circle.
3. Ask all students who remember their first day in the first grade to enter the circle. Again comment on their commonality. Return to large circle.
4. Ask all who remember what they dreamed last night to enter the circle. Again have them walk around. Ask them if they have been in the circle more than once, then have them go to the large circle.
5. Ask those who wish they were rich and beautiful/handsome to get in the center. Ask them to look around and see if there are people with them who were in the center before. Ask them if they see anyone new in the group.
6. Ask those who have only been in the center once to enter the circle again. (Most likely there will not be many; perhaps none.) If there are none, comment that it is not rare that they should have more than one thing in common with others in the group.
7. Process. "How did it feel when you discovered you had so many things in common with people that you thought were different from you?"

5.9 ARTIST AND BLOB

Materials: None.

Time: 10–15 minutes.

To the Teacher: This activity will help students relate to and relax with each other.

Directions to Teacher:

1. Have students seated in a large circle. Have them pair off with the person to their right into dyads.
2. Tell them one is to be the artist, one a blob. The "artist" forms his partner into some kind of statue. The "blob" relaxes as much as possible until the statue is formed. "Artists" give their works a name and share with each other. Then "blobs" become artists and do the same.
3. Process. "Does anyone have a work of art so fantastic they would like us to see it?" "How did you feel when you were the artist and could form the blob into something beautiful?" "How was it to be a blob, to have someone moving you around like that?"

5.10 PERSON-TO-PERSON ADJECTIVES

Materials: Copy of master 5.10, Person-To-Person Adjectives List, for every student.

Time: 20 minutes.

To the Teacher: The intent of this exercise is to help students clarify what they value in other people.

Directions to Teacher:

1. Explain to students that it is often hard for us to tell people what it is that we value in our friends. In this exercise students are to choose six words that are the most important things they value in their friends.
2. Hand out the list and give individual students ten minutes to choose six only.
3. Call time at ten minutes. Have students get in a circle of 6–10 students and share their six words. (As an option, if you have time, do all the sharing in one large circle.)
4. After everyone has shared, bring students into one large circle and discuss. "Do all our friends have all these qualities?" (The intent is to have students realize and verbalize that friends do not have to have all these qualities.) "If you value these in others, do you also value them for yourselves?" (Intent is to look at self values vs. what we value in others.)

5.11 THREE PEOPLE

Materials: None.

Time: 20 minutes.

To the Teacher: This activity will help students reflect on characteristics that are important to them in other people.

Directions to Teacher:

1. Have students get into groups of four. When seated, ask them to individually choose three people, still living, whom they would like to know. Give them two minutes to think quietly.
2. Ask students to share with their group the three people they chose and why they chose them.
3. After everyone has shared, in a large circle, process. "What was the strength the person had whom you wanted to know better?" "What does this say about how we choose people to know better?"

5.12 PAIR UP

Materials: None.

Time: 10–15 minutes.

To the Teacher: The purpose of this activity is to see how observant of each other students are, and perhaps how we communicate ourselves.

Directions to Teacher:

1. Have students form dyads.
2. Tell dyads to look very closely at each other, as though they were trying to "memorize" each other. One member of each dyad closes his or her eyes while the other changes something on his or her own person, such as untying his shoelaces. Then the observer opens his or her eyes and tries to identify the change.
3. Get students into large circle. Process. "Did you learn something about how observant, or unobservant, you are?" "What else did you discover about yourself during this activity?"

5.13 EPITAPH

Materials: Pencils and paper for each student.

Time: 10 minutes.

To the Teacher: The purpose of this activity is to help students focus on how they appear to others and what others think and feel about them.

Directions to Teacher:

1. Ask students, in groups of five, to draw a large tombstone on their paper.
2. Have students think for a moment or two about other people's opinions and feelings about them.
3. Then, following the example of the inscriptions on old tombstones, complete this line in fifteen words or less: "Here lies . . ."

4. Have students share their epitaphs, if they like, and ask other group members if what they have written is accurate according to the others' perceptions of them.
5. Process. "What did you learn about others' perceptions of you?" "How did it feel?"

5.14 DECLARING YOUR WANTS

Materials: None.

Time: 20–30 minutes.

To the Teacher: Implicit in many questions, hostile comments, resentments are "wants" the speaker has not been able to verbalize. This activity teaches students to declare straight-out what they want.

Directions to Teacher:

1. Have students in one large group.
2. Explain that many times we get angry at people because we haven't learned to simply state to them what we want from them or do not want. Ask the students: "What would make this class better for you? If you could make the people in this class do something to make it better for you, what would you demand we do? Begin your want: 'I want this class to . . . .'" (Get a volunteer to respond to that, then encourage others to do so.) After 2 or 3 students have done this,
3. Have students get into groups of 6 or 8. Have them practice declaring their wants of each other. Tell them to pick someone out, face the person, say his or her name and then make his or her want known. Emphasize to students that just as they do have the right to make demands of people, others also have the right to refuse their demands.
4. Process. "How did it feel to tell someone straight-out what you wanted or didn't want?" "Did declaring your wants work for you?" "Anything else anyone would like to say about this activity?"

5.15 EXPERIENCING TRUST

Materials: None.

Time: 30 minutes.

To the Teacher: The purpose of this activity is to help students realize there are various levels of trust and help students focus on their trust level in the group.

Directions to Teacher:

1. Before the session, write the following list on the board:
   - Imitate the crowing of a rooster.
   - Give a two-minute talk about your best qualities.
   - Do a silent pantomine of a sleepy person brushing his or her teeth.
   - Give a two-minute talk on what you like best about your classmates.
   - Recite a short nursery rhyme.
   - Balance a book on your head and walk across the room.
   - Read a short passage from any book in the room.
2. When students are seated, explain that the exercise will help them look at trust. Ask students to select the one activity they would most prefer to do and the one they would least like to do. Explain they may be asked to perform the task they selected as the one they most prefer to do.
3. When everyone has made their choices, by show of hands, note on the board the number of students that chose each option as number one.
4. In large group discuss the following: "How did you feel about the idea of performing?" "What relation might there be between people's choices and embarrassment?" "To what degree do you think your choice indicated your ability to trust others?"

5.16 HEAD LIST

Materials: None.

Time: 30 minutes.

To the Teacher: Be sure you have a relatively clean floor for students to lie upon. The purpose of this activity is to build trust.

Directions to Teacher:

1. Have students pair off in 2's.
2. Student A lies on his or her back and is to relax his/her head and neck.
3. Student B lifts A's head and rotates it gently for two minutes.
4. Reverse roles and repeat for two minutes.
5. Bring students back into one circle and process: "How did you feel, at first, giving control of your head to someone else?" "Did it get easier?" "Why?"

5.17 BLIND WALK

Materials: Blindfolds for half of the students.

Time: 30 minutes.

To the Teacher: In using this activity, be sure there is space for movement (i.e., hall, outside, gym). Its purpose is to help students get in touch with their trust level. Since students will be out of the room, check with the principal beforehand to explain what is going to happen.

Directions to Teacher:

1. Ask students to select one person they trust and go stand with him or her.
2. Ask the pairs to join into groups of 4, then 8, then 16, until the group is divided into two groups.
3. Ask one group to put on blindfolds.
4. Ask that each person in the other group select a blindfolded person and take him or her on a 5-minute walk. Stress they should be back in the room in 5 minutes and they should not disturb other classes. NO TALKING DURING THE WALK!
5. When they return, without discussion, have them switch roles for 5 minutes.
6. When they return, get everyone into a large circle for discussion. **(IMMEDIATE DEBRIEFING IS CRITICAL.)

   Debriefing questions:
   1. "How does this exercise relate to trust?"
   2. "Is trusting important?"
   3. "How did you feel when you were blindfolded? Were you trusting?"
   4. "How do you build trust?"

5.18 DEAR T.L.C.

Materials: None.

Time: 30 minutes.

To the Teacher: These letters are to be responded to by students. They are intended as a focus for discussion.

Directions to Teacher:

1. Have students organize into groups of five. Explain that you have received a letter addressed to "Dear T.L.C." seeking advice like Dear Abby. You will read the letter and ask each group to discuss how the group would reply.
2. Enforce a fifteen minute time limit.
3. In a large group, have each small group report on their responses.
4. Process learning.
      "In discussing the letter I learned..."
      (Have each student, in turn, complete the stem or pass.)

Letter 1:

"Dear T.L.C.,

I like this boy (girl) but don't know how to tell him (her). I find myself teasing and being sarcastic. I know there must be other ways to say 'I like you.' What do you suggest?"

Signed,
Ready to Move

Letter 2:

"Dear T.L.C.,

I'm getting ready to move to this new school and need to know how I can make new friends. What do I do to make new friends?"

Signed,
Moving

Letter 3:

"Dear T.L.C.,

I've been going with the same person for two years and he (she) now wants to break up. I'm afraid because I'm afraid I'll be lost without that 'one' person. What advice can you give me?"

Signed,
Break-up

5.19 POETRY/MUSIC "SELF EXPRESSION"

Materials: Record player.

Time: 25 minutes.

To the Teacher: Periodically, and as students want to, a time can be set aside for self expression.

Directions to Teacher:

1. Before this session, encourage students several times to bring poetry and music which says something about people and their relationships.
2. Have students sit in a large circle and explain that after someone shares his/her poetry or music, the group will discuss briefly (2-3 minutes) what the presentation was saying.
3. At the end of the session, ask students to complete: "Something I learned today about people was _____."

6

Developing Creativity

6.1 BRAINSTORMING

Materials: Sheet of paper and pencil for each group.

Time: 25 minutes.

To the Teacher: "Brainstorming" is an activity which enables group members to generate a vast number of alternatives. It also is an invaluable tool in tapping creativity of group members.

Directions to Teacher:

1. Have students get into groups of 5 and have each group select a recorder. Give paper and pencil to recorder.
2. Explain that one skill which helps groups function and come up with a lot of ideas is brainstorming. Explain the rules for brainstorming.
   (1) No discussion or judging!
   (2) Quantity, not quality, is most important.
   (3) Expand on each other's ideas, add on, "piggyback."
   (4) Record each idea, at least by a key word or phrase.
   (5) Set a time limit and hold strictly to it.
3. After students understand the rules explain that you are going to give them a task and they will have 3 minutes to come up with as many alternatives as they can. Say, "For the next 3 minutes I want you to brainstorm all the possible uses for a frisbee." After 3 minutes, call time and ask

each group to report out the number of uses of a frisbee they listed. Ask each small group to share with everyone a couple of their most creative ideas.
4. Tell students they have 2 minutes this time to brainstorm new and different uses for a skateboard. Remind them of the rules—quantity, no discussion, piggybacking on each other's ideas. After 2 minutes call time and have recorders report out as before.
5. Tell students that there'll be one more brainstorm. This time they're to think of all the things they as students can do to make school "better" for themselves. After 2 minutes, call time and let them share again.
6. Bring students back into a large circle to process. it feel to be able to say your ideas without being put down?" "How did the rules help you be more creative?" "How could we use brainstorming with other problems?"

6.2 KITCHEN UTENSIL

Materials: Each small group will need 6 toothpicks, 2 paper clips, 1 sheet of construction paper, 2 rubber bands and 1 popsicle or ice cream stick.

Time: 30 minutes.

To the Teacher: In this activity groups will work together to create a product.

Directions to Teacher:

1. Ask students to get in groups of 6.
2. Hand out a set of materials to each group.
3. Explain that great inventions are often the result of persons seeing things put together in different ways. Your group has a set of materials, and 15 minutes. Your task is to, *as a group,* make something that would be of use in the kitchen.
4. After 15 minutes, ask each group to share their invention.
5. As a large group process. "Was everyone allowed to be part of the group?" "How might you do the task differently next time?" "How did you feel about yourself in this group activity?"

6.3 MY INVENTION

Materials: None.

Time: 20–30 minutes.

To the Teacher: This activity is designed to elicit creativity from students.

Directions to Teacher:

1. Have students in small groups of 5 or 6.
2. Tell students that a recent news story on television told of a small town in Vermont which has become rather famous because 104 years ago a 15 year old boy, tired of wintry blasts of cold breezes on his ears, invented the first ear muffs. Then ask them to th ink to themselves, quietly, "If *my* hometown were to become famous 104 years from now because of an invention of mine, what would that invention probably be?" Give students about 5 minutes to think about the question, then ask them to share their inventions with their small groups.
3. After 15 minutes ask if some of the groups would like to share their "best" inventions with the rest of the class.
4. Process. "Would someone like to tell us how it felt to make your hometown famous?" "How did you feel about your invention, and sharing it with your group?"

6.4 TEAM PAINTING

Materials: Large sheet of poster paper plus crayons or felt-tipped markers in various colors for each small group. Masking tape.

Time: 30 minutes.

To the Teacher: This activity elicits creativity and encourages cooperation and teamwork from group members.

Directions to Teacher:

1. Have students in groups of 5 or 6. They may work around tables or on the floor. Give each group a large sheet of paper and a set of crayons or markers.
2. Tell students: "What you are to do is a team painting. Don't worry about your artistic talents! Each group is to work together on a team painting of 'How We Can Make School Better.' You'll have 20 minutes to do this, then you'll tape it to the wall and explain it to the rest of us."
   (*Note:* This may be combined with brainstorming, i.e., first brainstorm the subject, then do the painting.)
3. After 20 minutes, call time and have each group explain their team painting.
4. Process. "How'd you feel about your own contributions to your team's painting?" "What did you learn from this about your own part in making school a good place for you?" "Anything else anyone would like to share about all of this?"

6.5 IF I WERE A . . .

Materials: None.

Time: 30 minutes.

To the Teacher: This activity will help students focus on who they are, who they want to be, what they want to do. It will also help them see their uniqueness in contributing to their group.

Directions to Teacher:

1. Have students in groups of 5 or 6.
   Say, "I want for each of you to take a few minutes to think quietly to yourself, then share with your group 'If I were a piece of furniture I'd be _____ because _____!' Be sure and give your reasons for your choices! Any questions? Try to think about what piece of furniture best represents your own personality. You'll have about 10 minutes to do this." After 10 minutes (or longer, if it appears that more time is needed), say "Now I have another one for you. Remember, think to yourself quietly, then share, 'If I were a TV show, I'd be _____ because _____.'"
   After 10 minutes, call time.
3. Process. "What did you learn about yourself while doing this?" "Could someone share what you learned about someone else's personality today?" "Anything else anyone wants to say?"

Note: Other possibilities (or you may have better ideas of your own) are:

If I were an animal,, I'd be _____ because _____.

If I were a record . . .
If I were a tree . . .
If I were a part of speech . . .
If I were a state . . .
If I were piece of sporting equipment . . .
If I were a musical instrument . . .
If I were a vehicle . . .
If I were a building . . .
If I were a game . . .
If I were a toy . . .
If I were a flower . . .

6.6 I USED TO BE . . . BUT NOW I'M . . .

Materials: None.

Time: 20–30 minutes.

To the Teacher: The purpose of this activity is to help students think about how they have grown, their own responsibility for themselves, what contributions each can offer the group.

Directions to Teacher:

1. Have students in small groups of 5 or 6. Begin by saying: "I always used to (pause) but now I (pause). Can you think of something you used to be or do or think that has changed?" If the statements are incomplete, ask them to make them more complete. Then tell students to share in their small groups, one at a time, "I always used to be . . . but now I'm . . . ."
3. Process. "What did you learn about yourself?" "How did this make you feel about change, not staying the same?" "Anything else?"

6.7 UNIQUENESS

Materials: Drawing paper, construction paper, crepe paper, crayons, felt-tipped markers, stapler and paste for each group.

Time: 30 minutes.

To the Teacher: By creating their own artistic "masterpieces" and seeing that no two are alike, even though all used the same materials, students will be led to an appreciation of their own uniqueness and that different is not bad.

Directions to Teacher:

1. Begin by creating a piece of "art" in front of the class. Rip various colors of crepe paper into jagged shapes, staple or paste them onto the draw-

ing paper. Don't worry about your artistic skills! "Ham it up" and create your own masterpiece! When you're finished (5 minutes or less) ask: "Have you ever seen this before? One EXACTLY like this? What things can you say about this 'work of art' that are true? Do you know what 'creative' means?"
2. Lead students into a discussion of the impossibility of duplicating exactly what you did. Something that *"looks"* like yours could be created but it still would not be the same work of art.
3. Now say: "Now I want you to create your own masterpieces'." In groups of 5 or 6 share the paper and other materials and each person make his or her own work of art. You'll have about 10 minutes to do this."
4. After 10 minutes ask students to compare their "masterpieces" with the others in their group. Ask if any are the same.
5. As a total group, process. "We saw that each work of art in the class was one of a kind. Another word for that is 'unique.' Can any of these same ideas be applied to human beings?" Lead students to a gradual realization that each of them is different, each unique, each irreplaceable and impossible to duplicate.

6.8 TOTEM POLE

Materials: A sheet of poster board, six paper plates and multicolors of felt-tipped markers or crayons for each small group. Also, masking tape and paste.

Time: 30 minutes.

To the Teacher: Indian tribes used to make totem poles which were symbols of the things the tribe valued. They were creative works as well. In this activity groups use the totem pole idea to symbolize what they value.

Directions to Teacher:

1. Have students form groups of 6 and give each group a set of materials.
2. Ask students: "Do you know what totem poles are?" "Do you know what things were represented by the faces and designs on the totem poles?"
3. Explain that tribes are a kind of group as they are. Their task is to design and make a group totem pole symbolic of the things they value. Suggest they plan before they make.
4. Allow 20 minutes, then ask groups to put their totem poles on the wall and explain them.
5. As a total group process. "How did you feel about your own participation in this activity?" "How did you feel about doing what the Indians did?"

6.9 MAKE A DESIGN

Materials: Newsprint and marking pens for each group.

Time: 30 minutes.

To the Teacher: This activity helps students learn that group involvement can stimulate creative activities which lead to a productive outcome.

Directions to Teacher:

1. Have students in groups of 5 or 6. Give each group a sheet of newsprint and some marking pens.
2. Ask groups to draw a design on their newsprint with six blank areas large enough to contain a symbolic answer to the questions you have listed on the chalkboard as follows:
   a. What *one* quality do you prize most in friends?
   b. How do you show friends that you care about them?
   c. How do you share yourself with your friends?
   d. If you had *one* wish that could be granted for your school, what would it be?
   e. If you had *one* wish that could be granted for your school friends, what would it be?
   f. In the last block you can use words. Write three words which you would hope your friends would use in referring to you if you died today.
3. Draw a symbol which represents your group's answer to each question in a blank in your design. Art work doesn't count! The drawings can be simple, incomplete, not even make sense to others as long as the group knows what they mean.
4. After 15 minutes, share your design and symbols with the large group.
5. Process. "What did you learn about yourself in this activity?" "Anything else anyone would like to say about what we just did?"

6.10 NEWSPAPER SUPPORT

Materials: Newspapers, a roll of masking tape for each group.

Time: 30 minutes.

To the Teacher: This activity is one in which creativity is necessary to complete the task.

Directions to Teacher:

1. Have students in small groups of 5 or 6. Give each group a stack of newspapers and a roll of masking tape.

2. Tell students: "Your task is to build from the newspapers and masking tape something which will support the weight of one of the people in your group. You have 15 minutes to build your newspaper support."
3. After 15 minutes call time and have each group report on their task.
4. Process. "Did someone kind of become the leader in your group?" "How did you feel about your own participation or contributions?" "Did anything happen to slow you down?;;

Note to Teacher: In all probability the groups will report that the task was impossible. If this happens you may explain or demonstrate that by merely stacking the newspapers on the floor you can stand on them. Voila! They support your weight.

6.11 TOWER

Materials: For each group you will need 8 pieces of 8½ x 11 construction paper, a marking pen, 2 rubber bands, tape.

Time: 30 minutes.

To the Teacher: This activity helps students look at how they can work together as a group.

Directions to Teacher:

1. Ask students to get in groups of 6.
2. Hand out a set of materials to each group.
3. Explain that this is a contest. The products will be judged on the basis of *height, strength* and *beauty*. They will have 15 minutes as a group to build a tower.
4. Begin.
5. Stop after 15 minutes. Ask everyone to applaud according to how good each tower is in strength, height and beauty. The tower that gets the most applause will be the winner. Yelling will not count—only applause! (Be quick with this step.)
6. Process. "What did you learn from building your tower?" "How did you feel about the amount of applause your tower got?"

6.12 CREATE A GAME

Materials: Piece of paper and pencil for each small group.

Time: 30 minutes.

To the Teacher: Like tower building, this activity allows students to be creative in groups.

Directions to Teacher:

1. Have students in small groups of 5 or 6. Give paper and pencil to each group.

2. Explain that this is a contest to see which group can create the best game. The game must be played by at least 4 people. It will be judged on the basis of originality, creativity and simplicity. They have 15 minutes to create their game.
3. After 15 minutes call time. Have each group explain their game to entire class. After all games have been shared explain that judging will take place by applause. "We'll now judge the games. Applaud now for group 1 according to how original, creative and simple their game is. Now for Group 2 . . ., etc."
4. Process. "What did this game-making do for your own creative ability?" "How did the task progress in your group?"

6.13 WORDS INTO SYMBOLS

Materials: Drawing paper and multicolored markers for each student.

Time: 20–30 minutes.

To the Teacher: Intent of this exercise is to help students express ideas visually.

Directions to Teacher:

1. Draw a heart on the board. In a total group ask students what they think of when they see the drawing on the board (don't put a name to it). Write their ideas on the board by the heart.
2. Write the word "PEACE" on the board. Ask students what symbols/pictures they could draw that could depict "peace." Have students come draw them on the board.
3. Hand out paper and markers to each student. Explain that you are going to call out a list of words and that each student is to draw a symbol or picture representing that word. You will have one minute to do each drawing.
   ill
   healthy
   freedom
   truth
   your group.
4. Have each group member share his/her symbols for each word (each share on "ill," then each share on "healthy," etc.).
5. Ask each group to do a group drawing of their group (5 minutes) and share it with the total group.
6. As a large group, process. "How did this activity cause you to think differently about the words?" "How did doing the drawing of your group make you feel about members of your group?"

6.14 TWENTY WORDS

Materials: Pencil and paper for each group.

Time: 25 minutes.

To the Teacher: This activity encourages creative group behavior. Words used should be those that students are familiar with.

Directions to Teacher:

1. Before the session select a list of 20 words (see sample list) and write them on chalkboard so all students can see them.
2. Explain to students that they will be asked to do a task with the list of 20 words.
3. Ask students to get into groups of 6 and select one group member to act as recorder for the group. Give pencils and paper to recorders.
4. Explain to students that their task is to write a story using the 20 words in the order they are listed. They will have 15 minutes.
5. At the end of time ask groups to share their stories.
6. As a group, process. "How did you feel about your own participation in your group?" "How did the others respond to your contributions to the story?" "How did you feel about these responses?"

Twenty Words Sample List
   sun
   brown
   rowing
   dog
   table
   clock
   red
   cookie monster
   fly
   truth
   pencil
   Mandy
   nose
   motorcycle
   today
   light
   kitchen
   ball
   honey
   tomorrow

6.15 MAKE A STORY

Materials: Stack of magazines, scissors, paste, 1 piece of paper, pencil for each group.

Time: 30 minutes.

To the Teacher: The purpose of this activity is to elicit creativity from students. They may be told the stories will be given to some younger students (kindergarten).

Directions to Teacher:

1. Have students in groups of 5 or 6. Give each group a set of materials (listed above).
2. Tell students: "Today we are going to see how good you are at making a story for kids younger than you. Your task is to go through the magazines, cut out pictures and *easy* words and paste them on the blank paper so they tell a story. Make it something little kids would like! You have 15 minutes to do this."
3. Call time. Groups can share stories by trading them with each other until each group has read each story.
4. Process. "How did you feel about making a story for some little kids?" "What kinds of things about little kids did you have to keep in mind as you did this?"

6.16 T V SHOW PANTOMIMES

Materials: Card for each small group giving them the name of a popular T V show. (Suggestions: Mork & Mindy, The Dukes of Hazard, Happy Days, Mash, Hill Street Blues, etc).

Time: 20–30 minutes.

To the Teacher: This activity will enable students to see how creatively they can act and communicate nonverbally.

Directions to Teacher:

1. Have students in groups of 6-8. Give each group a card on which you have written the name of a popular T V show.
2. Tell students they are to think of a way to pantomime their T V show for the rest of the class. They *cannot talk.* They will have 10 minutes to decide how they will do this.
3. After 10 minutes (or longer if they seem to need more time) ask which group would like to "perform" first. No guessing what the show is until the pantomime is complete!

4. Process. "How did you feel about this activity?" "What kinds of demands did this pantomime put on you?" "What do you think we sometimes *knowingly* communicate non-verbally in groups?"

6.17 MAKE UP A LANGUAGE

Materials: A card for each pair of students, each card to have a statement on it (see list which follows).

Time: 20 minutes.

To the Teacher: The purpose of this activity is to elicit creativity from students.

Directions to Teacher:

1. Have students in pairs and tell them to face each other. Give each a card with a sample statement (see statements for "Make Up a Language") and caution them not to let partners see their cards.
2. Tell students they are to make up a new language. They should use completely nonsensical words. They have 3 minutes to think up a new language, then say their statements to their partners. Partners will have 3 minutes, then, to respond *in their own made-up languages* to what they *think* their partners said to them. After 8 minutes or so (when it appears that each dyad has completed its "dialogue") call time. Ask dyad member who had card to show it to partner.
3. Process. "How did you feel about speaking in your new language?" "What did tone of voice and facial expressions contribute to your understanding of each other?" "Are tone of voice and facial expressions as important as words?"

Statements For "Make Up A Language"

1. I like you. Will you be my friend?
2. Will you go to the football game with me?
3. Wow, it's hot today!
4. I just *love* hamburgers and french fries!
5. I feel so sad. My best friend just moved away.
6. I can hardly wait for Christmas!
7. She gave me an "F" and I'm so mad at her.
8. Want to skip class with me?

7

Making Decisions

7.1 BOMB SHELTER

Materials: Copies of master 7.1, Bomb Shelter, and a pencil for each student.

Time: 30 minutes.

To the Teacher: The purpose of this activity is to let students experience reaching consensus.

Directions to the Teacher:

1. Get students into groups of five each and hand out a printed exercise sheet to each student.
2. Read the situation to the entire group. Also read the descriptions of the people who are listed. Explain that consensus is not voting; it is discussing and coming to agreement.
3. Have each student check on his or her sheet the five who are to be saved. Say, "Remember, you are one of the six. You are choosing your companions for the next month."
4. Have each student tell his or her group the individuals he has chosen and why he or she made those choices.
5. Ask each group to come to a group decision on who they as a group would choose. All in the group must agree.
6. Each small group shares their decision with the other small groups.

7. Compare differences and similarities among groups.

Bomb Shelter
(To be read by Teacher)

One evening a year from now, you invite eight acquaintances to your home to talk with a psychology professor whom you know personally. In the midst of your discussion you hear the air-raid siren. You turn on your radio and the Civil Defense station broadcasts that enemy planes are approaching. Fortunately, you have a well-equipped bomb shelter in your basement, so immediately you direct the professor, your eight companions, and a mechanic who has been repairing the air conditioning unit downstairs, into the basement.

Shortly after you are in the shelter, a terrific blast shakes the earth and you realize that the bomb has fallen. For four frantic hours you get static on the radio in your shelter. Finally, you hear the following announcement: "A bomb has hit this area. It is of great magnitude; damage is extensive; radiation is intense. It is feared that all those not in shelters have suffered a fatal dose of radiation. All persons in shelters are warned that it would be fatal to leave before at least a month. Further bombing is anticipated. This may be the last broadcast you will hear for some time."

Immediately you realize that you have eleven persons in a shelter which is equipped with food, water and, most important, oxygen, enough to last eleven people for two weeks, or six persons for a month. When you reveal this information, the group unanimously decides that in order for anyone to survive, five must be sacrificed. As it is your shelter, all agree that you must stay and choose the other five who are to be saved. The ten persons are:

1. MARY, the psychology professor, is a few years older than the rest of the group. Others respect her and recognize her grasp of the situation and her ability to take control. Although she is rather cold and impersonal, she helped to quiet the group's nervousness and settled an argument between Don and Hazel. Even though no one seems close to her, you feel she would be valuable as an organizer and pacifier.

2. HAZEL is studying home economics, nutrition and dietetics. She is a very attractive girl. One of the first things she did was to appraise the food supply. You realize she knows how to ration food and avoid waste. Also, she's an imaginative cook who can fix even canned foods appealingly. She's efficient to the point of being domineering and bossy.

3. ALBERTA is a brilliant girl who has been given a graduate assistantship to do research on radiation. She has been pampered all her life and is horrified at wearing the same clothes for a month, being unable to take a bath or wash her hair, and sleeping in a room with five other people. Her scientific knowledge of the situation would help a lot; her whims and attitudes would be trying.

4. LAURA is a literature major who has read extensively and writes well herself. Already she has entertained and diverted the group by retelling one of the books she's read recently.

5. NANCY, Chet's wife, has a pleasant personality generally. However, she's been the most nervous and upset of the group. Her temperamental mood is partially due to the fact that she is expecting a baby in two months.

6. CHET, Nancy's husband, is a medical student. He has had two years of medical study, three summers in a camp as a medical director, and close association with his father who is a doctor. You realize he would be a great aid; however, he refuses to stay unless Nancy also remains.

7. JACK, the mechanic who has been working upstairs, also has a great deal of practical know-how. Although his education ended with high school, he has had experience with air-filtration systems, air purifiers and oxygen supply. He is a rather dull, chubby fellow. He has already been hassled by Hazel for taking a Hershey bar from the food supply. Despite his understanding of

the technical aspects, he fails to grasp the necessity for self control as far as the food and water supply is concerned.

8. PAUL, a young minister, is easy going. His calmness, optimism and faith are an inspiration to the group. He helped quiet Nancy's tearful outburst. At this time he revealed that he has learned to remain calm, of necessity, because he is a diabetic. He would require a special diet, and he easily becomes tired. Overexcitement causes him to faint.

9. JOE is a clean-cut, husky black football player, the star center of the college team. He is highly respected by everyone on campus. Joe was the only one able to lift the heavy metal plate that had to be placed over the shelter door. At one point, when Chet took it upon himself to set the oxygen tank valve, Jack flew at him, shoved him out of the way and reset the valve properly. A fight might have begun if Joe hadn't parted the two.

10. DON is a cheerful romantic. His smile, lively guitar music and sense of humor have helped improve everyone's mood. He gets along well with everyone but offended Hazel already by getting fresh. The others have also noticed his flirting eyes as he sings.

WHOM WILL YOU CHOOSE? Make your decisions and be prepared to give your reasons for having one person in preference to another. Remember, you are one of the six. You are choosing your companions for the next month.

7.2 NASA

Materials: Copy of master 7.2, NASA Worksheet, and a pencil for every student.

Time: 30 minutes.

To the Teacher: The purpose of this exercise is to demonstrate to students the value of group decision making. Usually group consensus yields a better score than individual scores.

Directions to Teacher:

1. Hand out a copy of NASA worksheet to each student.
2. Read the following to them: "You are on a moon probe. You are to rendezvous with your mother ship on the lighted side of the moon. Due to mechanical difficulties, your moon probe ship was forced to land 200 miles from your mother ship. When you were forced to land, much of your equipment was damaged. From the 15 items left, you are to choose the most critical. As an individual, number the items you think most critical with 1 and so on to least critical, numbering it

15. You will have 5 minutes.
2. After 5 minutes, ask students to get into groups of 5 and explain they will have 10 minutes to consensus* as a group on the most (#1) to least (#15) critical.

   *Explain that consensus is not voting, but is coming to agreement through discussion.
4. At the end of 10 minutes, stop the group; move into a large group. To score, have students fill in the NASA Ranking column with the rankings NASA astronauts came up with.
5. In the column marked "difference," have students write the difference between their number and the NASA number and add up their own scores and their group's score.
6. Process. "What did you learn about group vs. individual decision making?" (Most times the group will yield a lower score; for groups make better decisions than individuals do. This may be untrue if one person dominated or railroaded or if the group used a process other than consensus.)

7.3 HAVE TO, CHOOSE TO

Materials: None.

Time: 20 minutes.

To the Teacher: This activity demonstrates that students have more options than they often realize. In group work, persons often put limits on themselves that are not real.

Directions to Teacher:

1. Ask students to pair up with another student and sit so they can talk to each other.
2. Ask each pair to decide who will begin.
3. Explain that there are many things that we "have to do." Whoever begins spends one minute telling his or her partner all the things he or she has to do. Warn them they will use this list again and to remember what they are saying.
4. After one minute, switch and the other person lists all the things he or she has to do.
5. After one minute, ask the student who started to

Your Ranking	NASA Ranking	Difference		Group Ranking	NASA Ranking	Difference
	15	Box of matches				
	4	Food concentrate				
	6	50 ft. of nylon cord				
	8	Parachute silk				
	13	Portable heating unit				
	11	Two .45 caliber pistols				
	12	One case dehydrated milk				
	1	Two 100-lb tanks of oxygen				
	3	Map of moon's surface				
	9	Life raft				
	14	Magnetic compass				
	2	5 gallons of water				
	10	Signal flares				
	7	First aid kit containing injection needles				
	5	Solar powered radio receiver-transmitter				

Total number individual differences

Total number group differences

redo his or her list and say "I choose to" before each thing he or she listed as "I have to."

6. After one minute, switch and the other partner now does "I choose to."
7. In a large group process. "What did it feel like to say your "have to" as a "choose to?"

Variations: Following the same directions, substitute "I can't" and "I won't" for "I have to" and "I choose to."

7.4   CONSENSUS

Materials: Paper, pencil for each group.

Time: 30 minutes.

To the Teacher: Consensus and Brainstorming are two of the most valuable skills you can teach your students. Consensus is a solution agreed upon by all members of a group. Unlike "majority rule" it is a decision everyone in a group can live with or buy into.

Directions to Teacher:

1. Have students in groups of 5 or 6. Tell each group to select a recorder, then give pencil and paper to the recorder.
2. Tell students that each small group has been chosen to receive a pet guinea pig. The guinea pig is male. They have 2 minutes to brainstorm names for their guinea pig. Be sure recorder writes them all down! After 2 minutes, stop.
3. Explain that "consensus" is reaching a decision everyone can live with, that it is not like voting where some people win and some lose. In consensus everyone wins! The way to reach consensus is to go down their brainstormed list of alternatives (the names) one by one and cross out the ones no one likes. After this has been done, go down the list again—see if there are any other names they want to delete. Then go over the remaining suggestions, one by one, and decide on the one name they all can agree upon. (Remind students that this name may not be their favorite but it should be one they don't hate! One they can accept.)
4. Process. "Can you see other areas in which consensus might be helpful to know?" "How'd you feel about your group's choice of a name?"

7.5   CLASS GIFT

Materials: Pencil and paper for each group.

Time: 30 minutes.

To the Teacher: The purpose of this activity is to teach students the steps in decision-making.

Directions to Teacher:

1. Have students in small groups of 5 or 6. Give each group a pencil and a piece of paper.
2. Explain that each group is a special committee from their class, chosen by their teacher and classmates to select a class gift to their school. They have $250 which has been raised for this purpose. Tell students there are several steps in making decisions such as this. Teacher writes the steps on chalkboard:
   1. Define task.
   2. Identify alternatives.
   3. Evaluate alternatives.
   4. Select best alternative.
   Groups have 20 minutes to make their decisions.
3. After 20 minutes call time, have groups report to entire class on their selection.
4. Process. "What did you learn about yourself as you served on this committee?" "Was that the way you usually make decisions?"

7.6   DAVID CLASSMATE

Materials: A copy of master 7.6 "David Classmate," some crayons and a copy of the sentences to fill in (for David) for each group.

Time: 30 minutes.

To the Teacher: Students will make group decisions as to what kind of a person David Classmate is.

Directions to Teacher:

1. Have students form small groups of 5 or 6. Give each group a copy of the "David Classmate" pattern and set of crayons.
2. Say: "This is a new student in our class. His name is David Classmate. Give him some ideas that you feel would make him a nice person to know, one you'd like to have as a friend. Write his ideas in his head. Dress him in clothes. Give him some friends."
3. After 10 minutes give each group a copy of the incomplete sentences. Tell them to fill in the sentences for David. After they have done this,
4. Let each group share with the other groups their picture of David and their sentences.

7.7   TRIANGLE

Materials: One copy of master 7.7 Triangle worksheet, for each student.

Time: 15-20 minutes.

To the Teacher: This activity demonstrates that working in groups usually produces more accuracy than individuals can.

Directions to Teacher:

1. Hand out a triangle worksheet to each student.
2. Ask them to count the number of triangles on the page, keeping the number secret.
3. Ask students to pair up and jointly decide how many triangles there are.
4. Ask the pairs to get in groups of 6 (3 pairs); as a group decide by consensus (all agree) on the number of triangles.
5. Ask for each group to announce their findings. (There are over 45 triangles.)
6. As a total group process. "Did you find any difference between your intitial individual answer and the final group's answer?" "What does this say about using groups for decision making as opposed to everyone's deciding individually?"

7.8 FERNDALE TO AVONDALE

Materials: One set of master 7.8 Ferndale to Avondale cut-up clues for each group. (Note there are two sets. Set 1 is simpler than set 2).

Time: 30 minutes.

To the Teacher: In many groups, persons withhold information that could help the group with its task. This activity requires participant sharing in order to come up with the right answer.

Directions to Teacher:

1. Before class prepare a set of clues for each small group. (Set 1 is simple, set 2 is more complex.)
2. After students are in groups of 6, explain that each group member will be given several pieces of information necessary for the group to find the answer to how many wors it is from Ferndale to Avondale.
   Rule: You may share information but must keep your information slips in your hands.
3. Hand out a set of information slips to each group member.
4. After the groups have found the answer, process in their working groups for 5 minutes. "How did the group operate in making their decision?" "How might the group operate better next time?"
5. In a large group have groups share their conclusions.

Solution—set 1:
Ferndale to Lummi

1	4	litts		
3	12	litts per wor	=	2/3 wor

Lummi to Avondale

1	8	litts		
3	24	litts per wor	=	2/3 wor

Solution—set 2:
Ferndale to Blanco

5 bids		5	5
10 bids per wor		10	10

Blanco to Mason

10 bids		10	5
20 bids per wor		20	10

Mason to Ferndale

21 bids		21	7
30 bids per wor		30	10

17/10 wor = 1.7 wor

7.9 POSTERS

Materials: Newsprint, multi-colored marking pens, masking tape for each group.

Time: 30 minutes.

To the Teacher: The purpose of "Posters" is to help students learn to make decisions in groups.

Directions to Teacher:

1. Have students in groups of 5 or 6. Give each group newsprint, marking pens and masking tape.
2. Say: "What I want you to do is to make a poster by drawing a color, animal, symbol and slogan that represents your group. You'll need to really get your heads together on this, to decide together on which color, animal, symbol and slogan say it best. You'll have 20 minutes to do this. When you finish, tape your poster to the wall."
3. After 20 minutes have each group present and explain their poster.
4. Process. "How did your group do at making decisions together?" "Anybody learn anything about yourself which you can share with the rest of us?"

7.10 THE DECISION MAKER

Materials: One copy of master 7.10, The Decision Maker, and pencil for each student.

Time: 30 minutes.

To the Teacher: This activity will help students focus on the importance of some decision they will have to make during their lifetimes.

Directions to Teacher:

1. Have students in groups of 5 or 6.
2. Say: "Sometimes it is especially important to make a good decision, so people might get someone else to help them make these really important decisions. They might use a stockbroker, a lawyer, a doctor or an architect for certain difficult situations in which a decision has to be carefully thought out. When you have really tough decisions to make, you want experts to help you. Now, imagine a new kind of expert. Instead of a lawyer who is an expert in legal matters or a doctor who is an expert in medical knowledge, pretend there is a 'Decision Maker'—an expert on decision making. You can hire him to make your decision for you! The questions on the work sheet may help you learn something about yourself or about the decisions that are important to you. You have 15 minutes to fill out the work sheet, then you'll share it with your small group. Now I'll hand out the work sheets and pencils."
3. After 15 minutes call time and ask them to share their answers with their groups.
4. Process. "How hard or easy was it to decide what decisions to get help for?" "Did anyone have any particular problems with this activity?"

7.11 DECISION MAKING

Materials: Two extra chairs, 2 pieces of paper with circle faces drawn on, tape, 2 pieces of paper labeled "Temporary Member," 2 pieces of paper and 2 pencils for recorders.

Time: Two 30-minute sessions.

To the Teacher: This activity is divided into 2 parts, the open chair brainstorm one session and the role play in another session. In the role play the open chair is used to reduce the level of risk in exposing real concerns. The use of teams to play each role reduces the threat and the "Temporary Member" is a way to involve the outside circle.

Directions to Teacher:

1. Have students sit in a large circle, the 2 open chairs facing each other in the center. One chair is designated "boy," and the other "girl." Have boys in class (or half of class if numbers are uneven) group themselves around the "boy" chair, girls around "girl" chair. Say: "I want for all the boys to brainstorm for 4 minutes all the decisions that a boy your age might have to make during the next year of his life. One of you be recorder and write down all the decisions. At

the same time girls, you do the same thing. Brainstorm all the decisions that a girl your age might have to make during the next year of her life. And choose a recorder to write down all your ideas. Ready? Remember, you have 4 minutes to brainstorm."
2. After the brainstorming, the girls' list is read to the class, the boys listening carefully so they might add any ideas the girls' group missed. After the list is read, the boys' contributions are solicited and added to the list. Then do the same with the boys' list, the girls listening and then contributing their own ideas about decisions boys must make.
3. Now each group is asked to choose one decision from their list, one of particular interest to that group. (Teacher, you might draw a circle around the chosen decision on each list.) Discuss the nature of the decision, what kind of additional information might be needed and how to get it.
4. Role-play. Group decides on a situation in which two people would be involved in the decision (e.g., the boy has decided to drop off the basketball team and the coach needs him to stay). Or the situation may be one in which two alter-egos are arguing within a person (e.g., the girl is trying to decide whether or not to peek at her straight-A classmate's test paper which is in full view. The two roles are her own self arguing for and against cheating). The situations are role-played one at a time as follows: 3 volunteers are chosen to play each role. They group themselves on the floor around the chair that represents the role that they are playing, facing the other chair and the 3 other volunteers. The remainder of the class sits in chairs in one large circle around the 2 groups. A piece of paper marked "Temporary Member" is placed on the floor next to each group of volunteers.

7.12 CARO

Materials: Newsprint and marking pens or crayons, masking tape for each small group. Pencil and paper for each student.

Time: 30 minutes.

To the Teacher: This activity is designed to help students learn decision making skills.

Directions to Teacher:

1. Have students in small groups of 5 or 6. Give each group newsprint and marking pens or crayons. Also a piece of paper and pencil for each student.
2. Tell groups the following: "You are unhappy

with life here in the United States. The noise, confusion, tension, hassles and violence are getting you down. You have been discussing the possibility of finding a small island, far away from everything, where you can escape the problems here at home. A friend of yours feels he has just the kind of place you are looking for and gathers together a group of people, including yourself, who will be interested in making the move. A decision is made to leave the United States and and start a new life on this far-away island. The island is named Caro and a wealthy woman has donated a boat in which to make the trip. Since it's a small boat and you must take a supply of food, too, you may only take *one* suitcase. What I want you to do now is decide and list on your paper what belongings of yours you would take in your suitcase to this island called Caro. You have 10 minutes to do this and then share your list with your small group who accompany you."

3. "Now that you're all settled on the island of Caro you need to make a flag which symbolizes your new home. Use the newsprint and markers and create a flag which will symbolize to others what your island stands for."

4. After 10 minutes have groups tape their flags up and explain them to the large group.

5. Process. "What did you learn about yourself when you made your list?" "When your group made a flag?"

7.13 FIVE MORE FOR CARO

Materials: List of 8 people posted on newsprint or written on chalkboard.

Time: 20–30 minutes.

To the Teacher: This activity enables students to practice decision making and consensus.

Directions to Teacher:

1. Have students in small groups of 5 or 6. Post on front wall or write on chalkboard the descriptions of 8 people.

2. Say to groups: "You have learned there is room for five more people on the boat to the island called Caro. However, eight more people have asked to come along. The list here on the wall (or chalkboard) is a brief description of the 8 people who have asked to come along:
   • a 30-year-old white doctor.
   • a 60-year-old black minister.
   • a 28-year-old Mexican-American policeman.

• a 35-year-old black female singer.
• a white college student.
• a 34-year-old Oriental nurse.
• a 45-year-old white nun.
• a 20-year-old unemployed Vietnam veteran.

Each of you is to pick FIVE people from the 8 listed whom you would want to come on the trip. After everyone has done that, discuss your selections with your small group. Come to consensus in your group as to which 5 people should be picked. Remember, consensus means that your group's decision should be something each of you can live with! You have 15 minutes to make your individual selections, then reach consensus."

3. After 15 minutes, say: "Now each group will tell the other groups which 5 of the 8 people they want to take with them and why. Who wants to start?"

4. After each group has shared, process. "How did it feel to decide which 3 to leave behind?" "Was it hard for your group to reach consensus?"

7.14 TWO HEADS ARE BETTER THAN ONE

Materials: A copy of Master 7.14 work sheet you are using for each student. (Note: there are five different work sheets.)

Time: 20–25 minutes.

To the Teacher: The intent is to help students see that they make better decisions when they decide with others.

Directions to Teacher:

1. Before class select the work sheet you want to use and duplicate it for each student.

2. Hand out a copy to each student and ask them to individually rank the items listed in order, using the criteria on top of their work sheet. (For example, on the Drugs Work Sheet, put a 1 beside the drug that is most dangerous, etc.) Allow 5 minutes.

3. Post the correct ranking provided and as a total group process. "What did you learn about making decisions?" "What are the advantages and disadvantages of making group decisions by consensus?"

Note: Work sheet 4 may be shortened by limiting the number of proverbs. There is no correct answer to work sheet 4; it is only intended to focus on decision making by consensus.

TWO HEADS ARE BETTER THAN ONE WORK SHEET ANSWERS

Work Sheet 1
1 Alcohol
2 Barbiturates
4 Glue sniffing
5 Heroin
6 LSD
8 Marijuana
3 Speed
7 Tobacco

Work Sheet 2
8 15 feet of rope (keep all tied down)
7 Fishing kit (catch food)
3 5 gallons water (avoid dehydration)
9 Life preservers
12 Map of ocean (requires reading equipment)
13 Mosquito net (no mosquitos in ocean)
4 1 case C rations (food)
5 Plastic tarp (protection from elements)
14 Sextant (useless)
10 Shark repellent
1 Shaving mirror (signal rescue plane)
11 Transistor radio (unable to get distant signal)
6 Two chocolate bars (good energy source)
2 Two gallons gas/oil (signal)

Work Sheet 3
8 Begin or end school
9 Change in residence
11 Christmas
3 Death of close family member
1 Divorce
2 Jail term
5 Marriage
12 Minor traffic violation
7 Outstanding achievement
4 Personal injury or illness
6 Pregnancy
10 Vacation

Work Sheet 4
10 Auto repairman
2 Clergy
4 College professor
1 Doctor
8 Executive
3 Judge
5 Lawyer
6 Policeman
7 TV news reporter
9 U. S. Army General
11 Used car salesman

Work Sheet 5

There is no correct answer.

Authority

1: ranking by drug experts
2: ranking by seamen
3: research study of stress
4: university study of prestige

7.15   A OR B

Materials: One copy of master 7.15, A or B work sheet, for each student.

Time: 30 minutes.

To the Teacher: Often we are faced with deciding between two choices which look equally attractive. This exercise helps groups look at the consequences of decisions, as a way to make better decisions.

Directions to Teacher:
1. Ask students to get in groups of 4 and give a copy of the A OR B work sheet to each student.
2. Explain that their group has been given two options as to how they can spend a school day. Their task is to identify and list the costs and benefits of following each option, then as a group choose an option based on highest total benefit with lowest total cost.
3. Option A is spend the day at an amusement park. Option B is spend the day at a circus.
4. After 15 minutes stop the groups and if they haven't made a decision yet ask them to make one now based on the information they have generated.
5. Have each group report out their decision and cost/benefit reasoning.
6. As a total group process. "How can looking at the cost and benefits of two options help you in decision-making?"

7.16 PLEASE...NO! ...YES ... NO!

Materials: None.

Time: 30 minutes.

To the Teacher: Learning to say "no" is very difficult for many people. If they don't learn it, they may allow themselves to be walked over by others' expectations and desires. And if they can't say "no" and mean it their "yeses" are no more than conditional reflexes.

Directions to Teacher:

1. Have students in groups of 6 or 8. Tell them to pair up, to decide which of them will be A, which B. STOP RIGHT THERE and ask them to discuss with one another how the choice of who was A and who was B was made. "Is there a pattern in your life where you take the lead always? Or do you let others decide for you? If your partner had been of the opposite sex from what he or she is, would that have affected how your letter would have been chosen? Think about it!"
2. Now explain that the A's will be the please-sayers. They say *nothing* except "please." The B's each time are to respond with "No!" until the no-sayer (B) feels that the pleader has reached a deep sense of sincerity and humility in his request. Then he responds with "Yes!" Have partners change roles.
3. Process. "What was the most difficult thing about this activity?" "What did you learn about yourself as a please-sayer?" "How about as a no-sayer?"

Variations: Have the A's say "Yes!" and the B's respond with "No!" Let it develop into a lively two-word conversation using only the words "yes" and "no."

7.17 RANK ORDER

Materials: None.

Time: 15 minutes.

To the Teacher: This will give students experience in choosing from among alternatives and in publicly affirming and explaining their choices.

Directions to Teacher:

1. Explain to students that you are going to ask them some questions which will make them look inside themselves and try to decide what's important to them. You'll give them three choices each time and then you'll ask for two or three volunteers to tell you which is their first choice from the three, second choice and third.

2. Give an example: Teacher reads question: "Which do you like best?" then writes on the board:
   _____ jello
   _____ cake
   _____ ice cream
   Teacher tells students and writes 1, 2, 3 next to them, according to how he or she ranks the three choices.
3. Read question one, write three choices on board, and ask who would like to state his or her preferences. Ask if they would like to explain their choices. Then let one or two others state their choices and reasons. Try to get them to name their choices each time instead of simply saying "2-1-3" or "the same" so they will consider the alternatives carefully.
4. Go on to the other questions until you have only five minutes left.
5. Process. "How did you feel, having to decide what was most important to you out of maybe three things you liked?" "Did you learn anything about yourself in this exercise?"

Rank Order Questions

1. Where would you rather be on a Saturday afternoon?
   _____ at the lake
   _____ in the woods
   _____ at Winn's or the mall
2. Which is most important in a friendship?
   _____ loyalty
   _____ generosity
   _____ honesty
3. If I gave you $500, what would you do with it?
   _____ save it
   _____ give it to charity
   _____ buy something for myself
4. Which pet would you rather have?
   _____ a cat
   _____ a dog
   _____ a parakeet
5. Which would you rather be?
   _____ an only child
   _____ the youngest child
   _____ the oldest child
6. What would you be most likely to do about a person who has bad breath?
   _____ tell him or her directly
   _____ send him on her an anonymous note
   _____ nothing
7. Which would you rather have happen to you if you had bad breath?
   _____ be told directly
   _____ get an anonymous note
   _____ not be told

8. If you had a problem, to whom would you go?
   _____ parent
   _____ counselor
   _____ teacher
9. If there were a fight at school, where would you most likely be found?
   _____ in the midst of it
   _____ watching from the sidelines
   _____ going to find someone to stop it
10. Which kind of teacher do you prefer?
   _____ a nasty person but a good teacher
   _____ a nice person but a poor teacher
   _____ personality and teaching ability above average

11. What would you do if you saw your best friend steal some candy from a store?
   _____ tell on him or her
   _____ pretend you did not see
   _____ ask him or her to share it with you

12. Which is hardest for you to do?
   _____ show a bad paper to your parents
   _____ walk away from a fight
   _____ wait your turn when you have something you really want to say

(Teacher, you might like to make up some of your own.)

8

Solving Problems

8.1 UNIQUE DRAW

Materials: Drawing paper and markers for each group.

Time: 20 minutes.

To the Teacher: This activity will demonstrate the problem a group faces when confronted with an unclear task.

Directions to Teacher:

1. Ask students to get in groups of six.
2. Hand out a sheet of drawing paper and several markers to each group.
3. Explain that each group will have 5 minutes to draw something unique. Ask them to begin without further directions.
4. After 5 minutes, stop and process. "What made this task easy? Hard?" "What does this task tell you as a group about completing tasks given you?"

8.2 GROUP PROBLEM SOLVING

Materials: One copy of work sheet 8.2 Group Problem Solving, and pencil for each member.

Time: 30–45 minutes.

To the Teacher: This activity will enable students to work together to solve a problem. Let them know that this process is also useful when they are facing a problem of their own.

Directions to Teacher:

1. Have students in small groups of 5 or 6. Distribute pencils and one more work sheet than there are students in each group.
2. Tell students that each group will use only one work sheet, that each of them is to keep one for his or her personal use. Each group will choose a recorder to fill in the work sheet for their group. Explain that each group is to choose a problem to work on. It should be something in which they are all interested. An example might be that they don't have enough time in between classes, that the tardy bell rings too soon! After they have decided on a problem they are to work together on solutions, their recorder or secretary filling in the group's work sheet. Give them 20-30 minutes to do this.
3. After the work sheets are filled in have them share with the entire class the problem and solution they agreed upon.
4. Process. "Would someone like to share how you felt about this acitivity?" "How did you feel about your participation in your group?"

8.3   LETTERS

Materials: Paper and pencil for each group.

Time: 30 minutes.

To the Teacher: Part of being responsible citizens and students is not only to identify a problem but to try to do something about it. That is the purpose of this activity.

Directions to Teachers:

1. Have students in small groups of 5 or 6. Give each group some paper and a pencil and ask them to choose a secretary.
2. Tell students that they are to decide among themselves on a problem that is "bugging" them. Then they are to compose a letter to whomever they want—the President of the United States, the mayor, superintendent of schools, their principal—whoever they think has the authority to effect the changes they recommend. And if they would like to actually mail the letter you'll furnish a stamp! Give them 15—20 minutes to do this.
3. After the letters are written have each small group read their letter to the rest of the class.
4. Process. "How did you feel as you worked on your letter?" "Did you learn anything about yourself as you worked with your group on this?"

8.4   TINKER

Materials: A set of tinker toys for each group plus a set for a model.

Time: 30 minutes.

To the Teacher: This activity is designed to help students working in groups look at more effective group problem solving processes.

Directions to Teacher:

1. Before class use one set of tinker toys to build a model. The model should have 5 sections connected. (The intent is to show students that if they would discuss how to organize to solve the problem, they could work more effectively.)
2. Ask each students to get in groups of 5 and give each group a set of tinker toys.
3. Put your model where everyone can easily see it. Explain that the groups will have 10 minutes to replicate your model. Start.
4. Stop at 10 minutes and ask each group to describe how they approached the problem. "Did you jump in?" "Did one do it all?" "Did everyone go off on his or her own?"

5. Ask each group to discuss how they could complete the task more efficiently.
6. (Option) If time allows, you can give them 10 minutes to try again. (Dismantle what's already built.) Process. "How did you organize differently?" "How successful were you this time compared to the first? Why?"

8.5   SOUND BOX

Materials: A closed box with item, or items which will make an unfamiliar sound.

Time: 15-30 minutes depending on number of students.

To the Teacher: In problem solving it is of paramount importance to be able to recognize and/or identify clues.

Directions to Teacher:

1. Before class prepare a box by putting several items in it, so that when the box is moved it will make unfamiliar sounds.
2. Ask students to either
   a. form one large circle   or
   b. form an inner/outer circle.
3. Say: "I have a box here with several items in it. I will pass the box around the circle (or the inner circle) and you may shake it or do anything except open it. You are looking for clues as to what is in the box. You can keep the box only 30 seconds before you pass it on.
4. When the box has come back to you ask students what clues they have and what they think might be in the box.
5. Open the box and reveal what's in it.
6. Process. "What did this activity have to do with problem solving?" "How do you feel about the way *you* went about identifying what was in the box?"

8.6   TOY STORE

Materials: None.

Time: 20-25 minutes.

To the Teacher: This activity is a group problem which must be solved by consensus.

Directions to Teacher:

1. Have students get in groups of 4.
2. Say: "I am going to give you a problem verbally and your group is to solve the problem by consensus. I will feel free to ask anyone the solution and how it was arrived at."

3. Say: "The problem: you go into the toy store and buy a toy for $12.00. You give the clerk a $20.00 bill. Since the clerk doesn't have change, he takes the $20.00 bill next door and trades for 20-$1.00 bills, comes back and gives you $8.00 change and you leave. The guy from next door comes over to the toy store later charging the $20.00 was a phony and he demands $20.00 back. The toy store guy apologizes and trades the $20.00. Not counting the toy how much money did the toy store lose?"
4. When the groups have decided, ask each group to give their answer and explanation.
5. Ask the total group: "How did your group solve the problem?" "What did you learn about yourself as a problem solver?"

8.7 WHOSE PROBLEM IS IT?

Materials: Copy of master 8.7, "Whose Problem Is It?" work sheet for each student.

Time: 30 minutes.

To the Teacher: To be able to deal with a problem you need to recognize whose problem it really is. Often people will try to get you to buy into a problem that you're not part of.

Directions to Teacher:

1. Before class duplicate a copy of the "Whose Problem Is It?" work sheet for each student.
2. Ask students to form groups of 5 and hand out work sheets.
3. Say: "In order to solve a problem you need to be clear as to whose problem it really is. It could be your problem, other's problem or even external problems. Listed on your work sheet are 10 problems. Each of you decide for yourself whose problem it is and then come to group consensus (10 minutes maximum).
4. Post the correct responses and discuss, "Why is it important to recognize whose problem it is?"

Answers For Whose Problem Is It Work Sheet

Your problem
2, 3, 5, 10

External problem

Other's problem
1, 4, 6, 7, 8, 9

8.8 INTERVENTION

Materials: A copy of master 8.8, "Interventions Work Sheet," for each student.

Time: 30 minutes.

To the Teacher: When working in groups, situations arise which would interrupt the group process if someone did not intervene. This activity focuses on what to do in those situations.

Directions to Teacher:

1. Ask students to form groups of 6.
2. Say: "Whether you are a new group or old group, one concern you are faced with is how to deal with a situation that disrupts what the group is doing. In order not to be disrupted it is sometimes necessary to make an intervention.
3. Hand out work sheets and explain that the groups will have 20 minutes to decide how to handle each disruption.
4. In 20 minutes or after the groups are done, have groups report out how they handled each situation.
5. As a total group, process. "Which situation was most difficult to handle? Why?" "How would you feel if one of these situations happened in your group?" "Would you intervene—why or why not?"

8.9 HAPPINESS BOX

Materials: None.

Time: 15-20 minutes.

To the Teacher: Students will learn to work cooperatively in groups as they define a problem and arrive at solutions.

Directions to Teacher:

1. Have students in groups of 5 or 6.
2. Say: "I want each group to pretend that you can have a package any size or shape you want. Inside this imaginary box you are to place whatever it is in the whole wide world that would make our class happy. You have 10 minutes to do this, then I'll ask you to describe your 'happiness box' to the rest of us."
3. Call time and have each group describe the contents of their box to the rest of the class.
4. Process. "How did it feel to think you could make our class happy?" "Did your group have an easy time, or was it hard to decide on what went into your 'happiness box'?"

8.10 INSURANCE POLICY

Materials: Paper and pencil for each group.

Time: 30 minutes.

To the Teacher; This activity offers the students the opportunity to engage in creative problem solving.

Directions to Teacher:

1. Have students in small groups of 5 or 6.
2. Teacher introduces the concept of insurance policies for life, accident, fire, theft, etc., and notes that none of these policies actually prevents the occurrence of the disaster but merely offers money payments to counterbalance the disaster when, or if, it occurs. Then the teacher asks students to focus on the positive side of insurance policies. For instance, instead of taking out a policy against rain for the day of the class picnic there could be a policy that would provide for bright sunshine and temperatures in the mid-70's for that day!
3. Have students brainstorm for 5 minutes on special insurance policies they would like to see available. List them on chalkboard.
4. Have each small group select one policy from the brainstormed list on the board.
5. Have total group brainstorm for 3 minutes all the special conditions that could help sell their policy. (For instance, on the Eternal Life Policy special conditions might include eternal youth, vigor, wisdom, etc.)
6. After the special conditions brainstorm the group goes back to its original policy and brainstorms ways that this policy can be implemented. (For example, the Eternal Life Policy can be most nearly implemented by getting enough rest, exercising, eating the right foods, driving carefully, etc.)
7. Small groups report to each other on their special policies.
8. Process. "What did you learn about problem-solving as you selected an insurance policy?" "Can anyone share something you learned about yourself as you participated in this activity?"

8.11 WHAT'S STOPPING ME?

Materials: A large sheet of paper and a marker for each group.

Time: 20 minutes.

To the Teacher: This activity helps students look at factors which promote and inhibit problem solving using "force field" analysis techniques.

Directions to Teacher:

1. Ask students to brainstorm a list of problems they have as a group (e.g., too much noise during reading time).
2. As a group, select a problem which students have the ability to solve.
3. As a group, state the solution to the problem (e.g., room is quiet during reading time).
4. Ask students to get in groups of 6 and select a member to be recorder.
5. Ask groups to spend 3-5 minutes listing factors which promote our goal ("What factors promote a quiet room?").
6. Ask groups to spend 3-5 minutes listing factors which inhibit our goal (e.g., "What factors keep us from having a quiet room?").
7. Ask each group to select one inhibitor and list what the class might do to eliminate that inhibitor (e.g., open use of pencil sharpener anytime— might not allow pencil sharpening during reading since they're not supposed to be writing).
8. Report out and as a group discuss "What do you think of this way of solving a problem?" "When could this method be of help to you?"

8.12 FRIENDS

Materials: Paper and pencil for each group.

Time: 30 minutes.

To the Teacher: Loneliness is a real problem in schools. Many students do not know how to make and keep friends. This activity is designed to help them increase their skills in this area.

Directions to Teacher:

1. Have students in small groups of 5 or 6.
2. Explain that making and keeping friends is a problem to many students. What they are to do is brainstorm for 4 minutes in their small groups all the ways they can think of to make friends. Remind them of the rules of brainstorming. (You might write these on the chalkboard or post them on newsprint.) Tell them that after they do their brainstorming they are to pick what they think is their best idea and decide how to role-play it for the rest of the class. They have 15 minutes to do all this.
3. After 15 minutes call time and have each small group do their roleplay for everyone in the class.
4. Process. "Would someone like to share something you learned today about making friends?" "What did you learn about yourself in this activity?"

8.13 NEW KID

Materials: None.

Time: 30 minutes.

To the Teacher: A common problem is being new to a school or class where everyone already knows everyone else. Roleplay is a valuable tool for getting at the feelings of the newcomer and exploring his or her options.

Directions to Teacher:

1. Teacher draws a circle face on the chalkboard and writes under it "New Kid." Teacher explains that being new to a school or class where everyone knows everyone else can be a big problem. Ask how many of the class have ever been new. See if they will share their feelings about their experience. (Teacher might want to begin by giving one or two of his or her own experiences.)
2. After several students have shared some of their own experiences, ask if several would like to go stand by the face of "New Kid" and say some of the thoughts and feelings he or she might be having.
3. After random thoughts of "New Kid" have been expressed, draw another face on the board, this one "In-Group Member." Ask for volunteers to come up and roleplay "In-Group Member." Say what thoughts and feelings are going on in this student's head.
4. Ask "In-Group Member" and "New Kid" to talk to each other. If a student who is *not* involved in the roleplay has an idea about how to help "New Kid" make friends, he or she should join students who are "In-Group Member" and offer his or her ideas. Students not in roleplay should be encouraged, too, to step forward and offer any feelings they think "New Kid" is having.
5. After 15 minutes, process. "What did you learn about yourselves in this roleplay?" "Can someone share how you feel now about new students?"

8.14 I WISH I WERE...

Materials: Paper and pencil for each student.

Time: 30 minutes.

To the Teacher: After this problem solving session is completed it should be followed up for approximately 5 minutes once per week to allow the students to focus on the goals and behaviors they're working on.

Directions to Teacher:

1. Have students in small groups of 5 or 6. Give each student paper and pencil.
2. Ask students to write down three words which describe themselves. The words can describe them physically, emotionally, mentally or be personality or character traits. When they have done that ask them to turn the paper over and write three words they *WISH* described themselves.
3. After they have done this tell them they are going to take one of the three words on the second list and describe *specific* behaviors that kind of person exhibits. Give them an example—i.e., Donna says she wants to be friendly. What specific behaviors are "friendly?" Let students describe "friendly" behaviors. Explain that they are to share with their small group one of their words and the group is to help them with the specific behaviors. From the word they choose and the three or four behaviors the group helps them list they will choose a goal. Donna may decide that a specific behavior for "friendly" is to speak to other students before they speak to her. So her goal would be to do that and report back to her small group the next week on her progress toward being more friendly.
4. Tell them they have 15 minutes or so now to work in their small groups. The teacher should walk around and be available to help if students need it.
5. Process. "How did it feel to learn that you could start *now* to be the person you wish you could be?"

8.15 THE SCHOOL MURAL

Materials: Story and discussion sheet and pencil for each group.

Time: 30 minutes.

To the Teacher: This activity enables students to problem solve in their small groups. There should be a high trust level before this activity is introduced.

Directions to Teacher:

1. Have students in small groups of 5 or 6.
2. Tell students to listen carefully to the story, then they will get a sheet with the story and some discussion questions they will answer. Read story to class.
3. Hand out work sheet and pencil to each group. Tell them they have 15 minutes to answer the questions.

4. After 15 minutes ask which group would like to read their answer to the first question. Then ask for a response to #2, #3, etc. Try to get each group involved.

5. Process. "Would someone like to share any strong feelings you had about this?" "Was it easier to talk in your small groups because you trust each other?" "What did you learn about yourself from this activity?"

8.16 PROBLEM SITUATIONS

Directions to Teacher: The following are typical problems students encounter. They are included here as discussion topics.

1. Free Time. Jim had a stamp album, David was a sportscar buff, and Carol was learning to cook. John didn't seem to have any interests; and besides, he didn't seem to have enough money for a hobby. When he called on these children to play, quite often they said they were busy. John thought they were stupid, and said so. He said the only really interesting activity was sports, and why in the world didn't they see this and come out for a game of ball?

   Is there a right or wrong in this situation? What is an interest? Do you have one? Should you have one? Do people have similar interests? Should they? Are there any situations where people have similar interests? Are hobbies important? Will it be important in the future?

2. Learning. The 7th grade students at Bluff School have a learning problem. The teacher has made a spelling graph on which he puts the number of spelling words misspelled by the entire class. The children can then see if they are improving and how much they are improving as a whole class. The teacher is trying to get the children aware of their own progress and to try to improve. He has told the children that if they get less than five wrong in the total amount on the final test he would give them a treat. The problem arises in that there is one child who continues to get five wrong or more every week even though he is trying very hard. The children feel that they can never win as long as he is included in the group. However, the teacher has already told them that no one can be left out. Some of the children are beginning to put unfair pressure on the one child. They ridicule him and withdraw their friendship.

   Can you identify the total problem? Can you think of a good solution? Was this a good situation in the first place, since children are different? How should spelling be taught? Is it right for a teacher to give this kind of reward?

3. Responding. One of the paperback books used in the new materials in biology mentioned the process of plant and animal evolution. George wondered that if it were true about plants and animals, was it true about humans? The teacher's response interested the children. She said it was a question she'd prefer not to have asked or answered. She refused to discuss it any further, and that was that.

   What is the real problem here? Are there really questions that shouldn't be asked? Why did the teacher react as she did? What should George do?

4. Dating. Jane came to school and cornered Linda, Kate and Jenny, and stated proudly she had met a college sophomore and he'd taken her to lunch, and she had a date Saturday night for the drive-in. All of the girls were 15. Some of the group were envious, others thoughtful.

   Why were some envious? Why were some thoughtful? When should middle-school students begin dating? Should girls go with boys older than they? Should men and women discuss their dating situations? Can you write down other critical incidents concerning dating?

5. Special children. The special room within the orthopedic school contained eight brain damaged children having different ability levels. These children needed a very controlled, quiet atmosphere in which to work. One child within the class had severe emotional problems and screamed and yelled all day long. This child was made an outcast by the children because of her actions. This caused many problems because this child felt that the other children hated her, thus adding to her emotional difficulty.

   What is the problem here? If you were a teacher what would you do to help the children understand this child's actions? How could you help them accept her? How else do you work with disturbed people?

6. Bus. The school bus transported children on all elementary grade levels. One kindergarten boy was always trying to get the attention of a sixth grade boy on the bus. To get this attention he hit or poked him. One day the sixth grader shoved the kindergarten boy down in the bus, just to get him out of the way, and was reported to the principal. The kindergarten boy's father was also angry, and called the sixth grade boy's

father. All in all the sixth grader lost, yet felt he was right.

What is the problem? What are the ways the sixth grader could have given the younger boy some attention? Should parents get involved? What other problems can occur on a bus?

7. The sixth graders in Mrs. Wilke's class enjoyed her flexibility. She allowed freedom of movement, quiet discussion, a joke now and then, and gave blocks of free time for good work. Mr. Hays allowed no discussion, no movement within the classroom, and made a face at jokes. Jeff kept getting the two classes mixed up, and found himself in the office more than in the classroom, as he carried the freedom allowed in Mrs. Wilke's class into Mr. Hays' class. Eventually the class decided to help him. The next time Jeff was kicked out of class, they walked out as a group.

What is the real problem here? Should the class have approached Jeff alone, before the mass action? Is such action ever appropriate? Are there differences in room rules and should this be so? Who is in the right and who is in the wrong?

8. Fairness. Tom was a seventh grader who still had a reading problem, and even had walked home in anger from school the week before. On Monday, the teacher surprised the entire class by naming Tom as a patrol boy to fill in for a month for a boy who would be out ill for a long time. Paul was especially incensed. He'd been on his good behavior for years, and told the teacher so, just so he could get the opportunity to become a patrol boy. He thought it was quite unfair that Tom should be rewarded for being bad when he had not been rewarded for being good.

Why do you think the teacher did what he did? What do you think it will do for Tom? What do you think of Paul's reaction?

9. Life-planning. The fourth grade class at Black School created a new candy, and then set up a model factory and production line in the room to produce the candy. They planned sales and advertising campaigns and acted out completely

the kinds of things some of them would do as adults, and enjoyed the process thoroughly.

Is there something you can model like that? Is this a good way to practice reading or arithmetic skills? How else do you think the children could express their future roles as adults? Do you want to be an adult?

10. Grades. Don is a boy who has never been successful. His grades from his many classes have convinced him that he is not very good. He is bitter and feels that everything he does is useless. Consequently, he gives up and lives up to his reputation as a poor student, when in reality he could get A's in some subjects.

What should the teacher do? If he were given good grades as an incentive would it be fair to the other students? How should other students feel about Don? What could Bill do to help himself?

11. Acceptance. Park Junior High School was a friendly, warm place for most of its seventh graders. Some students, however, dreaded entering its doors. Judy was one of these, and some boys ridiculed her as she walked down the halls to her locker, calling her 'fats.' She never got angry, but she did get embarrassed.

Why are boys like this? Are people, not just boys, like this? Why is this so? Can Judy help herself? How can we stop this?

12. Popularity. Juan liked sports, Pam collected stamps, Maria played the violin and Jody sketched in charcoal. These hobbies were usually done out of school. Juan was on the basketball and track teams, Maria in the orchestra, but the other hobbies were not represented. Jody and Pam brought this up before the student council, stating they were unfairly treated as their hobbies were not represented in school activities.

Should all activities be represented in and out of school curriculum? Is one of these hobbies more important than the other? Is it good for someone to have an outside interest? Is this incident correctly titled?

9

Ending A T.L.C. GROUP

Just as it is critical to take the time to develop a sense of group when you begin a T.L.C., it is equally critical that you bring closure to a group.

The ending of a group can provide a powerful arena for learning or can give the group members an empty sense of loss. After one has invested many hours of him or herself in a group, it is the responsibility of the teacher/leader to end the group with the members feeling they have gained.

We have suggested only four activities for closing. Activity one should come first because it requires time for preparation. We suggest you do activity one, part one, four sessions before the end; then do the three activities suggested, and on the last day hold activity one, part two.

These culminating activities allow all to leave the group knowing the group was and will always be a part of their lives.

Directions to Teacher:
Part 1
1. Explain to the students seated in a large circle that the T.L.C. group has only four meetings left. You, the teacher, have planned for three meetings but not the fourth. You would like for the group to plan the fourth and final meeting. At each of the next three sessions you have set aside ten minutes for them to meet again.
2. Ask students to choose a group leader and allow that person to handle the remainder of the day.

(*Note:* To the extent possible, allow students a free hand. Whatever they decide to do will be theirs; value it.)

Part 2
On the final day, leave it in the hands of the student leader and enjoy.

9.1 ON OUR OWN

Materials: None.

Time: 30 minutes, part 1, 30 minutes, part 2.

To the Teacher: Activity one is designed to allow students to bring their own closure to the T.L.C. group, giving them the responsibility for goodbyes.

9.2 LEARNINGS

Materials: Pencil and paper for everyone.

Time: 20 minutes.

To the Teacher: The purpose of this session is to capsulate the learning of the T.L.C. group.

Directions to Teacher:

1. Ask students to divide their paper in four sections, heading each section as shown.
   Group: Communicating:
   Self: People-to-People:
2. Ask students for each to identify the most important thing they remember about that part of the course. Allow five minutes.
3. Ask students to get into groups of six and to share. Explain that after they share, they are to identify what is the most important thing they learned about working in groups.
4. After ten minutes, bring the students into a large circle and ask each group to share. If time permits, you may ask if anyone wants to share their individual learnings with the large group.

(*Note:* Be sure if you promised ten minutes for activity one followup, that you give them that time.)

9.3   FANTASY GIFTS

Materials: A box with everyone's name on a small slip of paper in it.

Time: 20 minutes.

To the Teacher: Through this activity students share in the giving. This activity is intended to help students look at the ending of T.L.C. as a celebration of happiness rather than a time of sadness.

Directions to Teacher:

1. Have students seated in a large circle.
2. Explain that people like to give and receive gifts of goodbye, celebration for holidays, etc. Since the group is going to say goodbye, you thought it would be nice to give gifts. However, since it is the giving, not the actual gift that is important, ours will be fantasy gifts.
3. Show students the box and explain that everyone's name is in it. After everyone has drawn a name, they will each have five minutes to decide on their fantasy gifts. Explain that the gift may be anything from a feeling to a thing. Allow

everyone to draw a name, including the teacher.
4. After five minutes, in a large circle, ask students to share their gifts.
5. After all gifts are shared, ask students how they felt, both in giving a gift and when they received a gift. If time remains, ask if anyone has another gift for anyone in the circle.

(*Note:* If you committed ten minutes for activity one, be sure they get it.)

9.4   WISHES

Materials: None.

Time: 20 minutes.

To the Teacher: Wishes are a way of saying goodbye. In this activity we give futuristic wishes to the group, ourselves, and another person.

Directions to Teacher:

1. Explain to the students that this session is on wishes. Say "We often in our lives have made wishes. Wishes we could do something, wishes for grades, wishes someone will get better, many wishes, each of which is a hope for tomorrow. Today we are going to make some wishes."
2. Have students pair up in dyads with someone to whom they would like to give a wish. Ask students to phrase their wish: "Something good I wish for you is _____." Allow 3-4 minutes for dyads to share their wishes.
3. Move into one large circle and ask students to make a second wish and share it with the group. "Something I wish for this group is _____." Allow everyone who wants to make a wish to do so, but do not require one.
4. Say, "Most important things we can wish for are for good things in our own lives. What is a good wish you would give yourself?" "I wish for me _____."
5. Process in large group. "Wishing makes me feel _____." Allow time for activity one if necessary.

Black Line Masters

Permission is granted by the publisher to individual purchasers to cut out and/or reproduce any or all of the material appearing on the following pages for use with the activities contained in this book.

Black Line Masters

1.1 HOW DO YOU SEE YOUR LEADER?

I as your leader am trying to improve my leadership skills. For each set of words mark the space that best describes how you see me as your group leader.

Example:

ORGANIZED ___ X ___ ___ UNORGANIZED

An "X" in the second blank means I am more organized than not but not completely organized.

CLEAR ___ ___ ___ ___ UNCLEAR

CONCERNED ___ ___ ___ ___ UNCONCERNED

FAIR ___ ___ ___ ___ UNFAIR

FLEXIBLE ___ ___ ___ ___ RIGID

FOCUSED ___ ___ ___ ___ WANDERING

HELPFUL ___ ___ ___ ___ UNCOOPERATIVE

NARROW-MINDED ___ ___ ___ ___ OPEN-MINDED

ORGANIZED ___ ___ ___ ___ UNORGANIZED

PREJUDICED ___ ___ ___ ___ UNPREJUDICED

PREPARED ___ ___ ___ ___ UNPREPARED

REASONABLE ___ ___ ___ ___ UNREASONABLE

RELAXED ___ ___ ___ ___ NERVOUS

SELF-CONTROLLED ___ ___ ___ ___ EMOTIONAL

WARM ___ ___ ___ ___ INDIFFERENT

1.2 PAY DAY CHECKS

Date _____ 19_____

Pay to the order of _____

Amount _____

for having done such a good job as a group member.

Date _____ 19_____

Pay to the order of _____

Amount _____

for having done such a good job as a group member.

Date _____ 19_____

Pay to the order of _____

Amount _____

for having done such a good job as a group member.

1.3 TELEGRAM

TELEGRAM   Date _____

To: _____

From: _____

Message: _____

_____

_____

==

TELEGRAM   Date _____

To: _____

From: _____

Message:_____

_____

_____

==

TELEGRAM   Date _____

To: _____

From: _____

Message: _____

_____

_____

==

1.7 PRAISE LIST

Good

Fine

Improving

Excellent

Good try

Correct

Nice

Much better

Good thought

Super

Superior

Very creative

Neat work

2.7 SELF ADJECTIVES LIST

Directions: From the list below, choose the six adjectives that best describe you.

able	efficient	nervous	self-conscious
accepting	energetic	noisy	selfish
aggressive	fair	normal	sensible
ambitious	free	organized	sensitive
annoying	friendly	passive	serious
bitter	gentle	perfectionist	shy
bold	greedy	pleasant	silly
brave	giving	questioning	sociable
calm	happy	quiet	stable
carefree	hard	radical	strong
careless	imaginative	realistic	stubborn
caring	immature	rebellious	tender
cautious	independent	rejecting	tense
clever	intelligent	relaxed	thoughtful
complex	jealous	reliable	tough
confident	kind	religious	trusting
conforming	lazy	respectful	understanding
critical	loving	responsible	vain
demanding	manipulative	rigid	warm
determined	materialistic	sarcastic	willing
dreamy	merry	self-accepting	wise

2.8 MY COAT OF ARMS

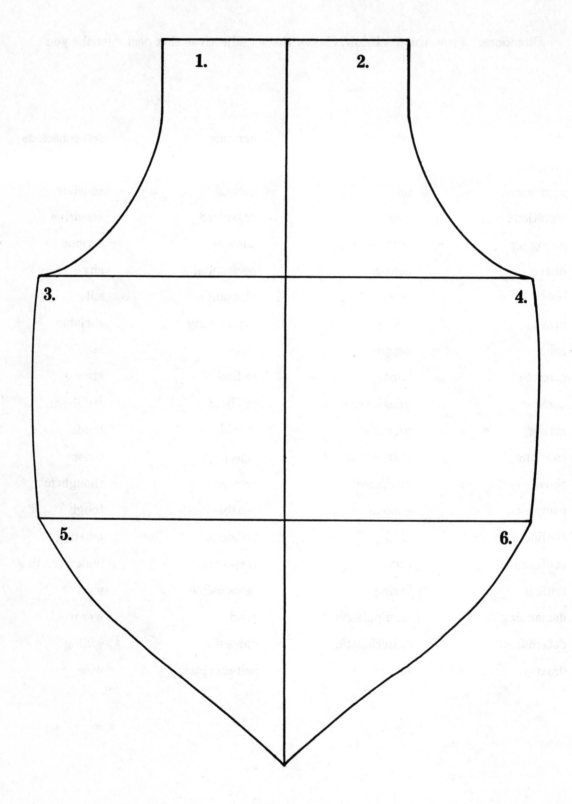

2.16 TWENTY THINGS

Name _____

Date _____

Things I Love To Do:	A/O	$	(−)	P	Week
1.					
2.					
3.					
4.					
5.					
6.					
7.					
8.					
9.					
10.					
11.					
12.					
13.					
14.					
15.					
16.					
17.					
18.					
19.					
20.					

2.21 PERSONAL INVENTORY

Fill in with at least two examples of each:

1. Experiences you have had so far:

   _____

   _____

2. Things you have done:

   _____

   _____

3. Ideas you have acquired:

   _____

   _____

4. Skills you have learned:

   _____

   _____

5. Values you have:

   _____

   _____

6. People you like or admire:

   _____

   _____

7. Places you have visited:

   _____

   _____

8. Books you have read:

   _____

   _____

9. Music you like:

   _____

   _____

2.22   AM I SOMEONE WHO?

Directions: Circle Y for "Yes," N for "No," and M for "Maybe." Be careful with the "Maybe's." Try hard to answer "Yes" or "No." If it's not something you do *now*, try to think ahead into the future when you might have to make a decision about it. Unless you feel very strongly that "Maybe" is your answer or will be, mark Y or N.

Am I Someone Who

1.	Needs to be alone?	Y	N	M
2.	Would let my child drink?	Y	N	M
3.	Judges others by how they look?	Y	N	M
4.	Can receive a gift easily?	Y	N	M
5.	Would let my child smoke pot?	Y	N	M
6.	Usually does well in school?	Y	N	M
7.	Is afraid to be alone in the dark?	Y	N	M
8.	Likes to get to know new people?	Y	N	M
9.	Likes the person I am?	Y	N	M
10.	Will put things off?	Y	N	M
11.	Talks loudly when nervous?	Y	N	M
12.	Always looks up a new word in the dictionary?	Y	N	M
13.	Would marry for money?	Y	N	M
14.	Likes to buy and wear new clothes?	Y	N	M
15.	Can express positive feelings toward others?	Y	N	M
16.	Could get hooked on drugs or alcohol?	Y	N	M
17.	Would like to become really well known?	Y	N	M
18.	Is known by others as "cool"?	Y	N	M
19.	Laughs a lot?	Y	N	M
20.	Can cry if I need to?	Y	N	M
21.	Falls in love easily?	Y	N	M
22.	Might donate my body for research?	Y	N	M

(Teacher, you might add some of your own.)

2.30 ALTER EGO PROFILE SHEET

Directions: If you were your alter ego, your other self, your free spirit, freed from all your present responsibilities, duties and relationships, what would you be like? Fill in your profile sheet and see.

1. Where would you live?

2. What would be your occupation?

3. List three hobbies you might like to pursue.

4. What foods would be on your weekly menu?

5. List three magazines that you would like to read.

6. What three books would probably be at your bedside table?

7. List three records, artists, or composers that would surely be among your record collection.

8. What kind of clothes would you wear, both for formal and casual wear?

9. Describe your home, both the outside and the inside.

10. What kind of car would you drive?

11. If you wish, describe the sort of person you would choose to marry. You may also list the names of several famous people, living, dead, or fictional, who would be among your closest friends.

3.10 PROVERBS

Cut on each black line

A stitch in time	saves nine.
A penny saved	is a penny earned.
A rolling stone	gathers no moss.
Haste	makes waste.
A watched pot	never boils.
An ounce of prevention	is worth a pound of cure.
The early bird	gets the worm.
Birds of a feather	flock together.
An apple a day	keeps the doctor away.
All's fair	in love and war.
Spare the rod	and spoil the child.
Fools rush in	where angels fear to tread.
A fool and his money	are soon parted.
Too many cooks	spoil the broth.
A new broom	sweeps clean.
When the cat's away	the mice will play.
Every cloud	has a silver lining.
Forewarned	is forearmed.
It is more blessed to give	than to receive.
Handsome is	as handsome does.

3.11 ROLE PLAY ROLE DESCRIPTORS

SITUATION 1: A, B Roles

SIT. 1.
Role A

You are at a school event talking with several friends. Close by someone you know is being loud and obnoxious. You walk over to him and he makes an embarrassing remark to you. What do you do?

SIT. 1.
Role B

You are at a school event. You are feeling lonely and want some attention. To get this you are being loud and obnoxious. A fellow student walks over and you insult his friendliness.

SITUATION 2: A, B Roles

SIT. 2.
Role A

You've been at school all day and every time you start to talk to your friend he/she just walks away. What do you do?

SIT 2.
Role B

You've been at school all day but aren't feeling well. You want to avoid people. Your friend walks up to talk to you. This is the fifth time today and you really want to avoid talking to anyone.

SITUATION 3: A, B, C Roles

SIT 3.
Role A

You have just watched two of your friends fighting verbally over what you supposedly told them. They come over to find out what actually was said. What do you do?

SIT. 3.
Role B

You've been fighting with a good friend over what a third friend said. You finally decide to go ask the third friend what he or she really said.

SIT. 3.
Role C

You've been fighting with a good friend over what a third friend said. You finally decide to go ask the third friend what he or she really said.

3.15 ACCIDENT REPORT WORK SHEET

Message: "Please listen carefully, as I must leave immediately to get to the hospital. I have just called the police from the principal's office here at school. Wait here and report the accident to them. As I was crossing the intersection, I saw a blue Volkswagen, which was heading east, start to make a right-hand turn when the gray '81 Buick, heading east, started to turn left. They must have both put their brakes on at the same time because both brake lights flashed on at the same time. The Buick's wheels must have locked because he crashed right into the side of the VW."

Directions: For each time the report is repeated, note any additions, subtractions or distortions from the previous report.

First repetition:

Second repetition:

Third repetition:

Fourth repetition:

Fifth repetition:

Sixth repetition:

4.10 STRENGTHS TARGET

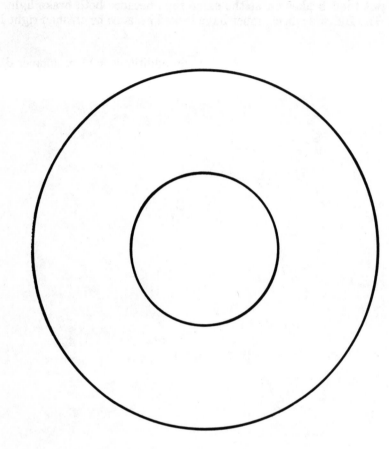

4.15 "BLOCKERS AND BUILDERS" ROLE CARDS

#1

You are negative about
any and all ideas

#2

You want your idea to
be the idea. You won't
listen to any others or
change your idea.

#3

You are positive about
all your ideas.

#4

You are the negotiator—
try to get everyone to
agree by compromise.

#5

You put down any ideas.

#6

You don't want to get
involved.

#7

Be yourself.

#8

Be yourself.

4.16 TURN ON, TURN OFF WORKSHEET

INDIVIDUAL

Words/phrases that
turn on

Words/phrases that
turn off

GROUP

Words/phrases that
turn on

Words/phrases that
turn off

4.17 "LABELS," SET 1

COMEDIAN:	laugh at my idea.
EXPERT:	seek my advice.
IMPORTANT PERSON:	defer to me.
STUPID:	treat me like I was a dummy.
LONER:	ignore my ideas.
OUTSIDER:	treat me with distrust.
HELPLESS:	give me positive support.
LOSER:	pity me.
STUTTERER:	what I say doesn't make sense.
OVER-EMOTIONAL:	comfort me.

4.17 "LABELS," SET 2

Listen to me and get me to talk.

Tell me I'm o.k.

Ask me about myself.

Yell at me.

Put me down.

Ignore me.

Look at my shoes as you talk to me.

Tell me I'm not o.k.

Talk at me when I'm talking.

Speak softly to me.

Don't let me say anything/you talk.

Back away as you talk.

Walk away in the middle of my talking.

Look into my eyes as I talk.

Help me.

Pity me.

Support me.

Reinforce me.

Stay away from me.

5.6 ROLE PLAY DESCRIPTORS

Directions: Duplicate and cut up. Each person participating will get role description.

SITUATION 1: A, B Roles

SIT. 1.
Role A   You are walking down the hall when you meet a very good friend. What do you do?

SIT. 1.
Role B   You are standing in the hall crying.

SITUATION 2: A, B Roles

SIT. 2.
Role A   You are in a noisy, crowded lunchroom. You see a person sitting by himself looking lonely. What do you do?

SIT 2.
Role B   You are new at school. You are sitting in a noisy, crowded lunchroom by yourself feeling lonely.

SITUATION 3: A, B Roles

SIT 3.
Role A   You are sitting in the cafeteria. Several students have been making cruel comments to another student. The student is hurt. You look over and catch his eye. What do you do?

SIT. 3.
Role B   You are sitting in the cafeteria. Several students just made some cruel comments to you which hurt you. You look over at a friend, looking very hurt, and you catch his eye.

5.10 PERSON-TO-PERSON ADJECTIVES

Directions: From the list below, choose the six adjectives that best describe what you look for in other people.

able	efficient	nervous	self-conscious
accepting	energetic	noisy	selfish
aggressive	fair	normal	sensible
ambitious	free	organized	sensitive
annoying	friendly	passive	serious
bitter	gentle	perfectionist	shy
bold	greedy	pleasant	silly
brave	giving	questioning	sociable
calm	happy	quiet	stable
carefree	hard	radical	strong
careless	imaginative	realistic	stubborn
caring	immature	rebellious	tender
cautious	independent	rejecting	tense
clever	intelligent	relaxed	thoughtful
complex	jealous	reliable	tough
confident	kind	religious	trusting
conforming	lazy	respectful	understanding
critical	loving	responsible	vain
demanding	manipulative	rigid	warm
determined	materialistic	sarcastic	willing
dreamy	merry	self-accepting	wise

7.1 BOMB SHELTER

Students: Check beside their names the five people you would choose to share your bomb shelter with you for the month.

1. Mary — Psychology professor, little older, good organizer and psychologist.

2. Hazel — Studying foods, cooks well, knows how to ration food but is bossy.

3. Alberta — Brilliant, radiation expert but spoiled and pampered.

4. Laura — Reader and writer, tells stories which keep people's minds off problems.

5. Nancy — Nervous, upset, expecting baby in two months.

6. Chet — Medical student with experience, won't stay unless wife Nancy stays.

7. Jack — Mechanic, knows air-filtration, etc. but no self control in matters of food and water.

8. Paul — Minister, inspires group but is a diabetic, faints when excited, needs special diet.

9. Joe — Football hero, black, very strong, kept Chet and Joe from fighting.

10. Don — Plays guitar and sings, sense of humor, flirts with the women.

7.2 NASA WORKSHEET

Your Ranking	NASA Ranking	Difference		Group Ranking	NASA Ranking	Difference
			Box of matches			
			Food concentrate			
			50 ft. of nylon cord			
			Parachute silk			
			Portable heating unit			
			Two .45 caliber pistols			
			One case dehydrated milk			
			Two 100-lb tanks of oxygen			
			Map of moon's surface			
			Life raft			
			Magnetic compass			
			5 gallons of water			
			Signal flares			
			First aid kit containing injection needles			
			Solar powered radio receiver-transmitter			

_____   _____

Difference your score and NASA   Difference group score and NASA

7.6 DAVID CLASSMATE

SENTENCES FOR DAVID CLASSMATE

1. I like _____.

2. I celebrate _____.

3. I am happy when _____.

4. I am sad when _____.

5. I'd like to grow up to be _____.

6. I enjoy _____ with others.

7. If I could have three wishes, they would be:

    a. _____

    b. _____

    c. _____

7.7 TRIANGLE WORKSHEET

Individual _____

Pair _____

Group _____

Class _____

7.8 SET 1

(CUT ON DOTTED LINES)

. . . .

How far is it from Ferndale to Lummi?

. . . .

How far is it from Lummi to Avondale?

. . . .

It is 4 litts from Ferndale to Lummi.

. . . .

It is 8 litts from Lummi to Avondale.

. . . .

Litts measure distance.

. . . .

Wors measure time.

. . . .

A person drives from Ferndale to Lummi at 12 litts per wor.

. . . .

A person drives from Lummi to Avondale at 24 litts per wor.

. . . .

7.8 SET 2

(CUT ON DOTTED LINES)

....

How far is it from Ferndale to Blanco?

....

How far is it from Blanco to Mason?

....

How far is it from Mason to Avondale?

....

It is 5 bids from Ferndale to Blanco.

....

It is 10 bids from Blanco to Mason.

....

It is 21 bids from Mason to Avondale.

....

What is a bid?

....

A bid measures distance.

....

How fast does a man drive from Ferndale to Blanco?

....

How fast does a man drive from Blanco to Mason?

....

How fast does a man drive from Mason to Avondale?

....

The man drives 10 bids per wor from Ferndale to Blanco.

....

The man drives 20 bids per wor from Blanco to Mason.

....

The man drives 30 bids per wor from Mason to Avondale.

....

7.10 DECISION MAKER WORKSHEET

1

Assume there are very few Decision Makers. You can assign only three decisions in your entire life to the expert. Which three would you assign?

a. _____

b. _____

c. _____

2

Assume you are required to assign *ALL* decisions in your life except three to the expert. Which three would you NOT assign?

a. _____

b. _____

c. _____

3

For each decision in question 1, what instruction would you give your Decision Maker? Why?

a. _____

b. _____

c. _____

7.14 TWO HEADS ARE BETTER THAN ONE

WORK SHEET 1

Rank the following drugs in order, from 1 being the most dangerous to 9 being the least dangerous.

Individual   **Group**

_____   Alcohol   _____

_____   Barbiturates   _____

_____   Cocaine   _____

_____   Glue Sniffing   _____

_____   Heroin   _____

_____   LSD   _____

_____   Marijuana   _____

_____   Speed   _____

_____   Tobacco   _____

7.14 TWO HEADS ARE BETTER THAN ONE

WORK SHEET 2

Rank the following in the order of their value to you if you were lost at sea in the Pacific Ocean. "1" would be most valuable, 14 of least value.

Individual   Group

_____   Fifteen feet of rope   _____

_____   Fishing kit   _____

_____   Five gallons of water   _____

_____   Life preserver   _____

_____   Map of the ocean   _____

_____   Mosquito net   _____

_____   One case of C rations   _____

_____   Plastic tarp   _____

_____   Sextant   _____

_____   Shark repellent   _____

_____   Shaving mirror   _____

_____   Transistor radio   _____

_____   Two chocolate bars   _____

_____   Two gallons of gas/oil   _____

7.14 TWO HEADS ARE BETTER THAN ONE

WORK SHEET 3

Many events in life cause stress. Rank the following as to how much stress they cause. Place a 1 next to the event that causes the the most stress through 12 causing least stress.

Individual   **Group**

Individual		Group
_____	Begin or end school	_____
_____	Change in residence	_____
_____	Christmas	_____
_____	Divorce	_____
_____	Death of close family member	_____
_____	Jail term	_____
_____	Marriage	_____
_____	Minor traffic violation	_____
_____	Outstanding personal achievement	_____
_____	Personal injury or illness	_____
_____	Pregnancy	_____
_____	Vacation	_____

7.14 TWO HEADS ARE BETTER THAN ONE

WORK SHEET 4

Rank the following jobs as to how trustworthy they are. Place a 1 next to the most trustworthy through 12 being the least trustworthy.

Individual   **Group**

Individual		Group
_____	Auto repairman	_____
_____	Clergy	_____
_____	College professor	_____
_____	Doctor	_____
_____	Executive of large corporations	_____
_____	Judge	_____
_____	Lawyer	_____
_____	Policeman	_____
_____	T V news reporter	_____
_____	Used car salesman	_____
_____	U. S. Army General	_____

7.14 TWO HEADS ARE BETTER THAN ONE

WORK SHEET 5

Listed below are proverbs. Rank them as to their importance in life; place a 1 beside the most important, a 2 beside the second most important, etc.

Individual		Group
_____	A stitch in time saves nine.	_____
_____	A penny saved is a penny earned.	_____
_____	A rolling stone gathers no moss.	_____
_____	Haste makes waste.	_____
_____	A watched pot never boils.	_____
_____	The early bird gets the worm.	_____
_____	Birds of a feather flock together.	_____
_____	An apple a day keeps the doctor away.	_____
_____	All's fair in love and war.	_____
_____	Spare the rod and spoil the child.	_____
_____	Too many cooks spoil the broth.	_____
_____	Every cloud has a silver lining.	_____
_____	Don't put off till tomorrow, what you can do today.	_____
_____	It is more blessed to give than to receive.	_____
_____	Honesty is the best policy.	_____

7.15 A OR B WORK SHEET

Option A is _____   Option B is _____

_____   _____

Benefits	Costs	Benefits	Costs

8.2 PROBLEM-SOLVING WORKSHEET

Directions: Please answer each of the following questions by writing your answers in the blank spaces.

1. What are some of the problems or conflicts you are facing right now?

2. Choose one of the problems or conflicts above that you would like to work on. Explain it in more detail here:

3. What do you see as some of the possible solutions to the problem? (List as many as you can think of.)

4. For each of the above solutions fill in the grid and list the positive (good) and negative (bad) outcomes that might result from that solution.

Solution	Positive Outcomes	Negative Outcomes

5. Which solution do you think is most worth trying?

6. What might be some of the barriers you would meet in trying this solution? What steps would you need to take to remove or deal with these barriers? List below.

Solution	Barriers	Actions to Overcome Barriers

7. Do you want to try your solution? If so, what steps will you take and *when* (dates) will you take those steps?

8. What was the outcome of your efforts?
   (Fill in later.)

8.7 WHOSE PROBLEM IS IT?

WORK SHEET

Listed below are 10 problems. For each, decide if it is your problem, the other person's problem or an external problem.

Your problem. e.g., what to do Saturday.
External problem. e.g., hurricane hit India.
Others own the problem. e.g., Tom and Sue are breaking up.

_____ 1. A student tells you she is bored with school.

_____ 2. Your parents say you have to go with them regardless of previous plans.

_____ 3. A friend comes over and frequently takes your books from where they belong and leaves them lying around.

_____ 4. Your best friend has been moping around since her boyfriend moved away.

_____ 5. A friend has been using your library card to check out books.

_____ 6. A friend cries when she doesn't get her way.

_____ 7. Your friend's mother complains that her son isn't getting homework done.

_____ 8. A friend in your class complains that he's been smoking for years and can't quit.

_____ 9. A friend blows his top and tells you how much he hates you and the world.

_____10. Your friend comes over in the afternoon while you're trying to get chores done.

8.8 "TEN OCCASIONS FOR GROUP INTERVENTIONS"

WORK SHEET

Directions: In your small group, you are to discuss how you would handle the following situations. You have 20 minutes to decide on appropriate interventions you might make. You will be asked to share your interventions with the large group.

1. A group member speaks for everyone. ("Manny, we feel you're being unfair to Joe" or "We think we ought to . . . .")
2. An individual speaks for another individual in the group. ("I think Kay is getting angry at you, Manny" or "Well, what I think Joe is trying to say to this group is . . . .")
3. A group member focuses on persons, conditions or events outside the group. ("They shouldn't even let people like that teach. You know what she did to a friend of mine yesterday?" or "It's just impossible for me to please my mother. No matter what I do, it's not good enough. For instance, ...")
4. Someone seeks the approval of the group leader or a group member before and after speaking. (Member looks at group leader both before and after speaking to assess if he has leader's approval or agreement. Or "Isn't that the way you feel, too, _____?")
5. Someone says, "I don't want to hurt his feelings, so I won't say it."
6. A group member suggests that his problems are due to someone else. ("I feel like people dislike me because they know my Daddy is a policeman" or "Well, when your mother's an alcoholic like mine you have to expect your friends' mothers to be suspicious of you.")
7. An individual suggests that "I've always been that way" or "That's just the way I am and I can't help it."
8. An individual suggests, "I'll wait, and it will change."
9. Discrepant behavior appears:
   a. Between what a member is currently saying and what he said earlier.
   b. Between what a member is saying and what he is doing.
   c. Between what a member says and what he feels.
   d. Between what a member is saying and what the leader is feeling in reaction.
   e. Between how a member sees himself, according to his own data, and how others in the group have been seeing him, according to data they have at one time or another proffered.
10. A member bores the group by rambling.

8.15 THE SCHOOL MURAL WORK SHEET

THE SCHOOL MURAL

The mural has hung for years in the foyer of Valley View High School. The painting was there long before the school became desegregated. It shows persons belonging to several ethnic groups engaged in various kinds of work. Blacks are shown working in a cotton field.

This morning Superintendent Goodfellow received a call from Harold James, the high school principal, informing the superintendent that he had been visited by a group of Black students demanding that the mural be removed on the grounds that it is offensive to Blacks. The principal and the superintendent are both aware that the white community regards the painting as a tradition and a work of art.

Discussion Questions

1. What is the problem?
2. Is there a basis for the Black students' objection to the mural?
3. What are the possible reasons for their objection?
4. Should the mural continue to hang in the desegregated school?
5. What alternatives do the superintendent and principal have?
6. What would you do?